MANAGING THE GAME:
THE OFFICIAL'S OFFICIAL GUIDE TO CONTROLLING PRESSURE SITUATIONS

Over 1600 quotations about managing conflict.

MANAGING THE GAME:
THE OFFICIAL'S OFFICIAL GUIDE TO CONTROLLING PRESSURE SITUATIONS

Over 1600 quotations about managing conflict.

John Laurie

BY DR. JOHN LAURIE

MANAGEMENT LESSONS COMPILED FROM 45 YEARS OF QUICK DECISIONS UNDER TOUGH CIRCUMSTANCES

Copyright 2008 by Dr. John Laurie
Printed in the United States

All rights reserved by author

ISBN 978-1-58597-458-0
Library of Congress Control Number: 2007943532

4500 College Boulevard
Overland Park, Kansas 66211
888-888-7696
www.leatherspublishing.com

Why Read This Book?

The main purpose of this book is to more clearly understand some difficult Management situations through the eyes of an administrator and sports official, using football officiating analogies as metaphors.

The second purpose is to share information with all sports officials, offering strategies and suggestions to increase their interest and improve their skills in their positions.

John Laurie

Acknowledgements

There are nine people that I would like to personally thank for their help with this book:

ROXIE BYRNE, *Draft Typist, Village Presbyterian Church, Prairie Village Kansas*

MARILYN BREWER, *Editor Blue Valley West High School, Communication Arts teacher, Overland Park, Kansas*

GRACE CORRICK, *Editor, Blue Valley West High School, Media Specialist, Retired, Overland Park, Kansas*

RUAN HARTIS, *Editor, Blue Valley West High School, Secretary, Overland Park, Kansas*

ADAM HOFMANN, *Photographer, University of Kansas Student, Lawrence, Kansas*

CINDY HORCHEM, *Editor, Piper High School, Journalism Teacher, Shawnee, Kansas*

KAY LAURIE, *Editor, Sister-in-Law, Topeka, Kansas*

MICHELE ROOK, *Art Director, Leathers Publishing, Overland Park, Kansas*

STEVE THOMAS, *Cover Design, Creative Art Director, Camp David, Overland Park, Kansas*

Dedication

I would like to thank the hundreds of officials, teachers, and administrators that I have had the opportunity to work with through my vocation in education and avocation of sports officiating. I believe my philosophy and beliefs related to leadership and management are enhanced through my experiences as an educator and sports official.

I would like to dedicate this book to my parents, Dave and Gerry Laurie, who still live in my hometown of Atchison, Kansas. Dad was a big influence in the sports careers of my two brothers, Dave and Phil (active football official in the Big XII Conference); and my mother was the driving force for keeping the importance of getting a good education always at the front and center of our family goals.

I would also like to thank my wife Jeanette, for her patience and understanding through my constant research for materials; as well as, recognize my four boys: Kurt, Kip, Kelly and Chad. I hope Jeanette's two children, Kim and Todd, will enjoy the book as well as (some day) our six grandchildren: Klaire, Khloe, Jackson, Cy, Jacob and Connor.

Introduction

This compilation of material represents what happens when you put small pieces of paper in a folder and choose to not review them for a number of years. When I would hear someone say something that could result in a quotation about officiating, I would simply write it down and then at some point try to make "football officiating sense" out of the idea. I then started my collection of quotation books, which numbers over 200, doing the same thing; reading something and then seeing if I could apply a word or two, or possibly a concept into the field of sports officiating.

It was at this point that I found a good use of quotations by sharing them with Big 8 and now Big XII football crews the day before the game. As a referee, I would ask each official to pick three quotations (at that time I had about 100) to discuss with the crew the following day about two hours prior to the football game (during what we call "pregame"). I was pleasantly surprised how "open" the crew of officials became about discussing the quotations that they chose. These men have very strong egos. It appeared that by having a quotation in their hand, they found it much easier to discuss a "weakness" that they were going to try to improve upon by simply sharing a quotation. Interestingly, I have used the same method in high school and college classroom settings with the same positive results.

How to use this book if you are not a sports official

Don't be fooled by all of the "football officiating" language. Each section of the book has a reminder that the intent of these messages go far beyond the football field. It is the author's hope that you will transcribe the football "lingo" into a business, home, or even personal reference to get the full meaning of the book.

If you decide to use this book in the business world, I would like to challenge you to use the book the way the author did with his football crew. Share some of the material with your business associates, have them pick a statement or two, then openly speak to defend or reject the quotations they have chosen. You will be amazed at the openness and frank discussions that will follow.

A special note to Sports Officials

The concept of using this material was originally designed to create "conversation" among football crew members to discuss either something about themselves, others, or the "perfect world" related to football officiating. Good sports officials have a lot of confidence in themselves and in what they do, or they could not be consistently effective. Picking out a few statements that are important to them to share in conversation with crew members during their meeting time (pregame), I have found to be very valuable and insightful. It has helped officials express themselves in important ways, not only to themselves but also the crew. It has also given me important information (good and not so good) about each official. There is something about having a "crutch" (a football related statement) to share with others, that is made more comfortable in their hand while they discuss their philosophy related to the topic. I can assure you, this is an excellent technique to use with a football crew, and office group or even your family.

A Corporate Leaders' Perspective of this Book

"The principles that John has laid out in this book will make you successful in officiating or in business. As a C.F.O. and also a crew-mate with John for three years I saw him stress the simple tenants: teamwork, communication, preparation, accountability. He was able to do this in a fun and productive way with his crew. Put these principles to use and you will be successful in whatever you do."

His material does remind me of my thoughts as to why being a C.F.O. of a public company (under a lot of scrutiny since 2001) is much like being a college example. Here are a few examples:

1) *A good crew consists of GOOD people. It is no different in business as it all starts with having the right people.*

2) *PREPARATION. As in business, you must prepare yourself mentally and physically for every day. You must feel prepared in order to be confident on the field or in the business office.*

3) *As in business, we have a RULE BOOK, but a lot of the calls that we make are subjective. If we play exactly by the rules nothing would ever happen, there would be a penalty every play...same in business.*

4) *TEAMWORK and COMMUNICATION. If you think you can be successful in the business world by not being a team player, you are wrong. As an official, if you are not looking out for the crew (your team) you will not be a part of the crew for long. If you can't communicate you will not be able to get everyone pulling in the same direction.*

5) *As in business you have a ROLE to play, and you must rely on others to do their job. However, if you can help to save the crew, or help the company, you do.*

6) REVIEW PERFORMANCE on a timely basis. In football it is weekly; in business it is stock price. However, the faster you learn and correct the better.,

7) If you BLOW A CALL or make a bad move in business, you will be criticized. You must have confidence that you are doing the right thing and stick to the plan. If you let the naysayers influence you, you are lost.

8) ADAPTABILITY. You will have a team (officials or business) where everyone is very different. However, you band together for a common purpose.

9) GUILT BY ASSOCIATION. Being on a football crew, or being a partner in business brings about successes and failures; effective officials and business leaders always come together in crisis and realize that the view of the whole is always more important than the parts.

10) If you want to EXCEL in business or as an official, you must be competent, pay your dues, be a team player, and take the "heat" as you move up. Even more importantly, you must be selfless and approachable, while hopefully being mentored by someone that can help you to be noticed and recognized.

Jim Hatfield, SVP & SFO, OGE Energy Corp., Oklahoma City, Oklahoma.

— *30 years football official (WAC, Big XII, 84 games, four bowl games including the Rose Bowl).*

Endorsements

"Read this book once; review many times, you'll be a better official."

— Tim Millis
Former Big XII Supervisor of Officials

"To me John Laurie epitomizes the dedication, leadership, and the talent to have been one of the finest of the corps of men who serve as officials for modern day, big-time athletics. He earned the respect not only of those with whom he worked, but also from those for whom he worked. I have been blessed to have been able to watch him in action for many years."

— Max Falkenstein
KU Hall of Fame Sports Announcer

"A lot of wisdom, humor, insight and helpful tips that will be instructive for not only officials but others as well. This book would not only be helpful to officials, but also useful to leaders in all areas. As a public speaker, this book has provided me with a lot of material that I plan to use in the future."

— Dave Armstrong
TV/Radio Announcer: Big XII,
ESPN, Colorado Rockies and
K.C. Royals Baseball Teams

"John Laurie is as fine a man as I have had a chance to work with in officiating. He has been an excellent football referee certainly because of his individual skills and judgement, but his real strength is his determination to do everything he can to make members of his crew successful. I learned so much in the time I spent with John about football and about life in general. This book is a reflection of his continued interest in trying to make football officials better."

— John Robinson
WAC, Big XII and NFL Football Official, High School Assistant Principal; Bountiful, Utah

"Great material for the sports official and those in the business world."

— Red Cashion
Retired NFL Referee

"Humorous antidotes with a message to sports officials and business leaders."

— Paul Brown
Retired Big 8 Official, Attorney, Omaha, NE

"John, you are among the 5 great college referees that I have known, and consider insight you provide in your book to be invaluable in sports officials and business leaders."

— Randy Christal
Southwest Conference, Big XII Conference Referee, Public Relations Consultant, Austin, TX

"I think the idea for your book is great, and I remember some of the comments from your past pre-games. I enjoyed the "shots" you took at the referee position."

> — Hal Dowden
> Big 8, Big XII Conference Referee,
> Wister, OK

"I wish you great success with your book. Congratulations on your effort on this task and all of your other accomplishments."

> — Phil Luckett
> NFL Official

"Excellent material for the fan, official and those in leadership positions."

> — Al Green
> Big 8, Big XII Official, Executive
> Sales, Columbia, MO

"Your book brought back many, many memories. You were clearly one of the top three referees (30+ years) that I have ever worked with; particularly in terms of pre-game preparation, on the field decorum and game administration."

> — Frank Gaines
> Retired Big 8 Official, IRS retired,
> Lincoln, NE

"When I was reading your book, it brought back a ton of memories and game situations. I always enjoyed your pre-games and looked forward to seeing some of the quotations in your book. I learned a lot from the philosophy you used as a referee in my business, and I believe that many of the antidotes in this book apply directly to the business sector."

— Jim Jankowski
Retired Big 8, Big XII Football
Official, Business Owner
Waterloo, NE

"While reading this book, many ways came to mind as to how it could be put to use; and not the least of which is the entertainment for the 'uneducated' in sports reader. I think every aspect of this book's content would provide a great enlightenment to all new sports officials, prior to their first step into competition. Also, the book will provide officials with experience and opportunity to have a little 'light-hearted' continuing professional education before and during their season. For myself, the book will provide an opportunity to reflect on the good times with the great people with whom I came in contact with during my tenure as a football official."

— Bobby Ratliff
Retired Southwest Conference
Football Official, Retired IRS,
Hvurst, TX

TABLE OF CONTENTS

Section 1 — Coaches 1

Section 2 — Communication 31

Section 3 — Confidence 57

Section 4 — Good Officials 69

Section 5 — Humor 93

Section 6 — Leadership 139

Section 7 — Loyalty (Teamwork) 155

Section 8 — Mechanics 173

Section 9 — Philosophy 187

Section 10 — "Poor Officials" 265

Section 11 — Pregame 281

Section 12 — Referees 297

Section 13 — "Rule Book" Officials 319

Section 14 — Supervisor/Observer/Umpire 329

Section 1

Coaches

Oklahoma/Nebraska conversation.... Coach Osborne asked to use my mic. He requested that the "Great fans of Nebraska not throw oranges on the field" (Orange Bowl tradition) or he would support an unsportsmanlike penalty for their behavior. After this statement he asked me if I had turned my mic off? I told him "Yes" and his response was: "Don't you dare penalize us!"

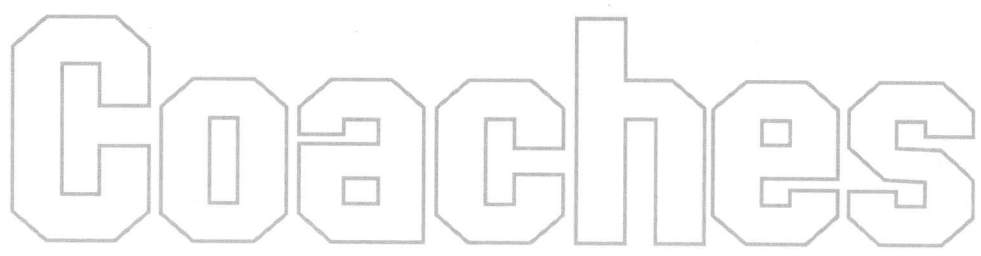

Coaches

I have officiated high school and college football for over 40 years. I have been a school teacher and administrator for over 45 years; so I have a great deal of respect for sports officials. Some of my very best friends and some of the people that I admire most in life are high school and college coaches. Some of the quotations I have prepared are simply "tongue-in-cheek" and make fun of a very small part of the coaching profession. You will also notice that I take some "fun" shots at officials and supervisors; of whom I also have the greatest respect.

One of the most difficult things for an effective referee to do, when in a heated conversation with a coach, is to be silent even when you know you are right.

◆

One way to keep a simple conversation from being boring is to say the wrong thing.

◆

When you are confronted by a coach, just remember that you are either the hammer or the anvil.

◆

Getting even, making up a call or showing a player or a coach up, is the last refuge of an incompetent official.

It is not a bad idea, as you walk toward a coach for "one of those visits," to spend about 30% of your time thinking about what you are going to say — And about 70% of your time thinking about what he is going to say to you.

◆

Your officiating career is in the hands of any player or coach who can make you lose your temper.

◆

Many times it is not the truth that you and the coach are yelling about, but simply each of you trying to persuade the other.

◆

When visiting with a coach, it is better to admit you are wrong and correct things than to win an argument with a lie.

◆

In all coach/official interactions, there needs to be one acting as the professional adult, and it always works out best on the field if it is the official.

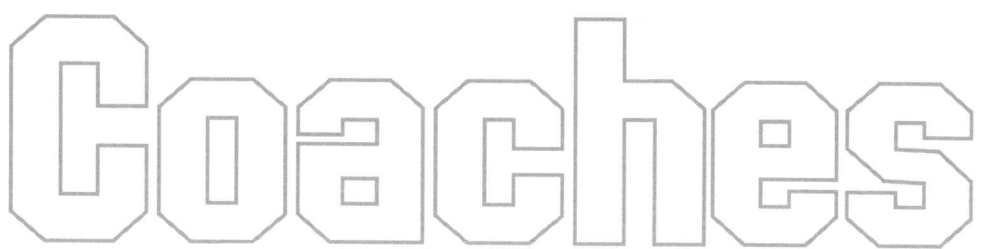

Never put a coach with a 911 problem on hold.

◆

I have noticed that nothing I NEVER said to a coach or player ever got me in trouble. ✓

◆

The best coaches find a way to control their emotions by application of reason and rules to their argument.

◆

Everything that irritates us about coaches can help us to better understand ourselves.

◆

Winning an argument with a coach does not mean you win.

◆

You can tell a clever coach by how he answers questions. You can tell a wise coach by his questions. ✓

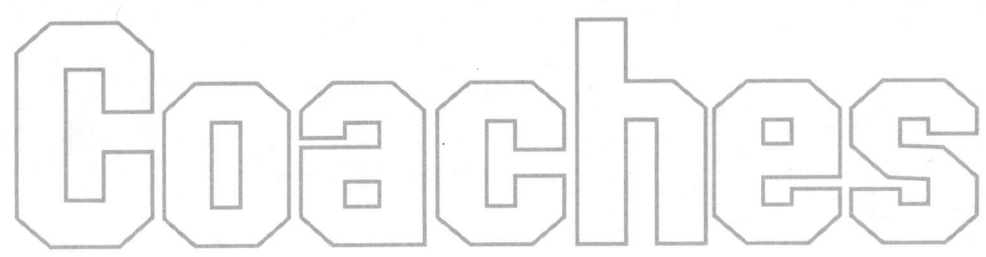

The perception of some visiting coaches when they step on the field for a big game is that the guys in "stripes" have acquired the same high degree of prejudices they had last week when they were the home team.

◆

If you have never been hated by a coach, you have never been an official.

◆

Some coaches simply have "frozen anger." Don't expect them to warm up after the first kick-off. Let it go and officiate the game.

◆

To carry a grudge against a coach or a team is like being stung to death by one bee.

◆

When in a confrontation with a coach, it is not how NEAT your uniform — But the expression on your face that is the most important.

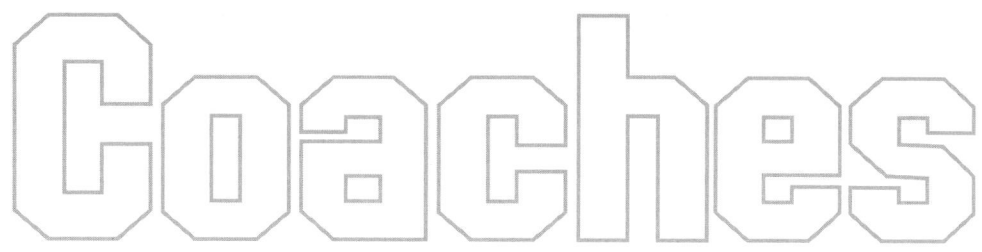

Coaches

If you are in an argument with a coach and you are not sure who the jerk is — You're it.

◆

If you don't know the rules and you are trying to discuss a situation with the coach — You might as well have both feet firmly planted in the air.

◆

A coach once told me, "If I start blaming the officials for the things that happen on the field, I have just given my team a perfect excuse to lose."

◆

When confronting a coach who is very upset, yelling and waving strong gestures toward you, try to remember the Chinese proverb "Outside Noisy-Inside Empty."

◆

If you think the coach has nothing to argue about — You are still in an argument.

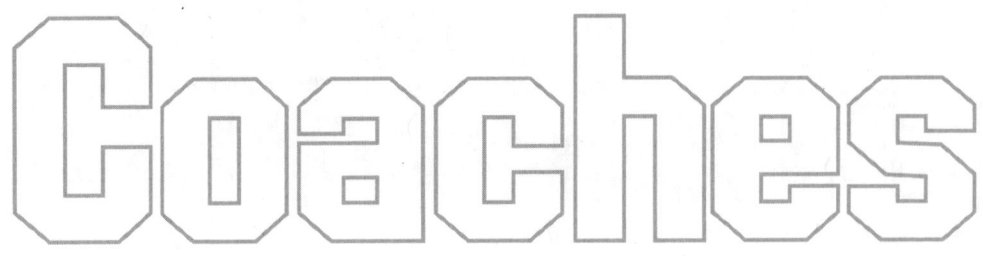

You will be making a mistake if you confuse a coach's actions on the side line, with his coaching and professional thought. Avoid this "first impression" when it is time to visit.

◆

Every coach has the right to be heard, but not ALL of them need to be taken seriously.

◆

The only sure way to tell if a coach is upset with you is to watch his face. If his lips move, he is upset with your performance.

◆

The best intentions and honest perceptions when explaining a situation to a coach, if exaggerated, weaken your position and credibility.

◆

The greatest conversation with a coach is finding mutual agreement! The key is finding that moment and then leaving quickly. (Hopefully you won't hear much about your ancestry as you move away.)

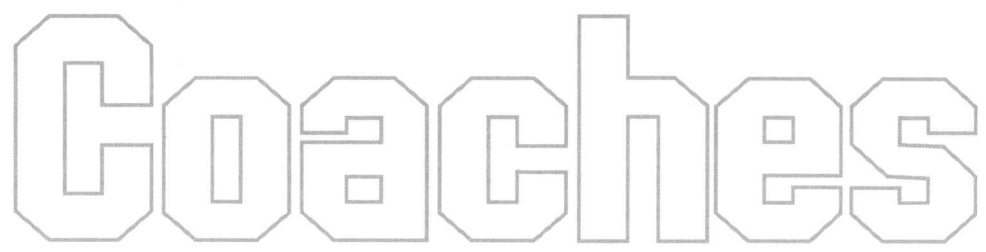

Coaches

If you try to please ALL of the coaches ALL of the time, you will make most UNHAPPY, MOST of the time.

When a coach is losing, it is your responsibility to not take it personal or personally.

If the coach is having a bad day, make sure he is the only one with this problem.

When visiting with a coach, remember that the reverse side also has a reverse side.

In a confrontation with a coach, the best way to leave the situation is to see how quickly you can agree on one point, and then leave quickly.

Coaches and officials who mistrust the most, should be the least trusted.

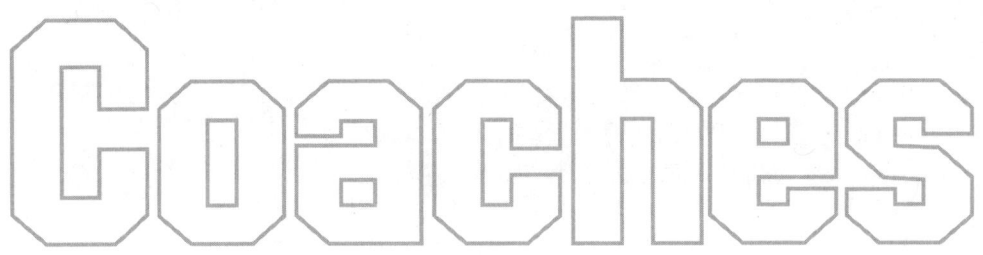

Coaches

<u>Politeness</u> during a difficult conversation with a coach can have a almost magical effect which can result in a positive conclusion, even though the differences of opinion may remain. ✓

◆

Tell the coach exactly how you feel when you are angry, and you will make the very best statement you will ever regret.

◆

The next time you are ready to put the coach in his place, try putting yourself in his place.

◆

When confronting a coach, first work to understand followed by being understood.

◆

When visiting with a coach, his level of respect for you is lowered when you raise your voice.

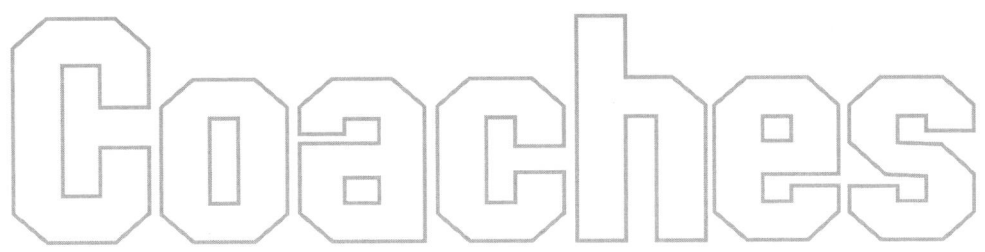

Coaches

The greatest "smart ass" comment that I have ever made to a coach was the comment that I chose NOT to make.

◆

You can suffocate a simple explanation to a coach by using too many words.

◆

Say to the coach what you are required by rule to say; not what you would like to say.

◆

You will seldom lose a conversation with a coach if you are totally honest, kind and professional — As well as a good listener —Just don't stay too long. ✓

◆

The art of a successful conversation with a coach is knowing when to stop.

◆

Expecting a coach to treat you politely, because you are a "good" official is like expecting the bull not to charge because you are a vegetarian.

The coach who upsets you the most is your best teacher, because he brings you face-to-face with who you are.

◆

Avoid coaches whose mascots are birds. They will cover you with their wings and peck the hell out of you with their beaks. (For my Jayhawk friends.)

◆

Beware of a coach who has nothing to lose.

◆

To simply do the opposite of what a coach wants is also a form of intimidation!

◆

Even though it may not show, it is difficult for a coach to not respect you if you are kinder than necessary.

◆

It is not a bad idea when visiting with the coach, to pick battles big enough to matter and small enough to win.

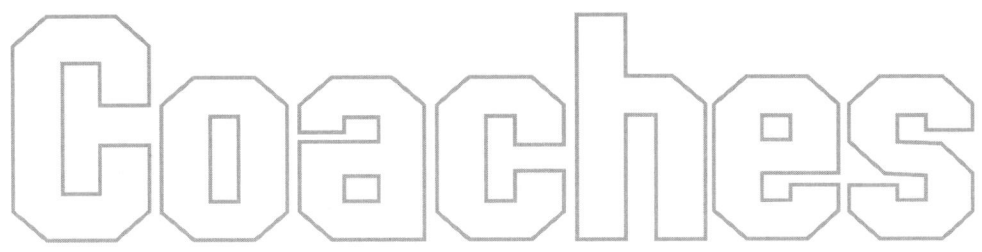

Nothing annoys an out-of-control coach as much as forgiving him and moving on.

―――◆―――

If a coach is ignorant of the facts, you can't win the argument. If the facts aren't in his favor, be brief and leave.

―――◆―――

When dealing with a difficult coach, it is better to know some of the questions than ALL of the answers.

―――◆―――

In order to manage a difficult coach, you must first manage yourself.

―――◆―――

Saying the right words to a coach may be very effective, but saying nothing at the right time can be more effective. ✓

―――◆―――

The coach who has the ability to anger you, has also conquered you.

Coaches

The key to visiting with a coach is to determine if he has something to say or whether he is simply trying to say something.

◆

The greatest disrespect you can show a coach is to use your authority and reject or support something that you know nothing about.

◆

Coaches give the perception that they only want what is "right and fair." The problem develops when you understand that what they want is not "right or fair." ✓

◆

Coaches will often ask the wrong question. It is your job, regardless, to give the right answer to the situation!

◆

<u>Strong</u> language comes from weak coaches and officials. ✓

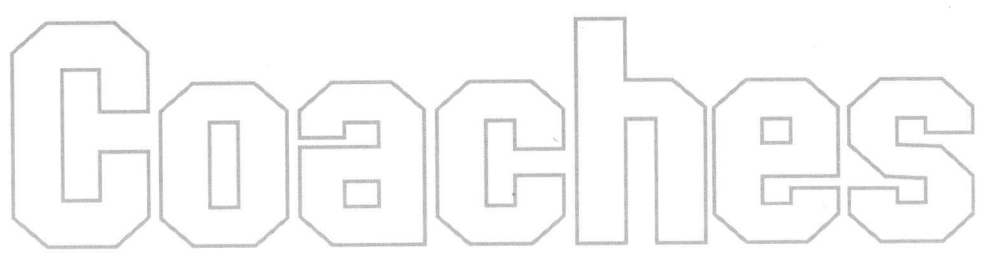

Coaches

Officials are lenses through which coaches read their own minds. So if a coach accuses an official of cheating, who is really the "cheater"?

―◆―

When visiting with a coach, his choice may be more "emotion" or "show" than sincere questioning — Which is of course his "choice."

―◆―

When a coach agrees with everything you say, he is either a fool or he is getting ready to skin you.

―◆―

There is a level, when dealing with an irate, disrespectful coach, that you draw the line and protect your sacredness of self-respect.

―◆―

Generally, the more you say to a coach, the deeper the emotional hole you enter. The fewer the words, usually the better the understanding.

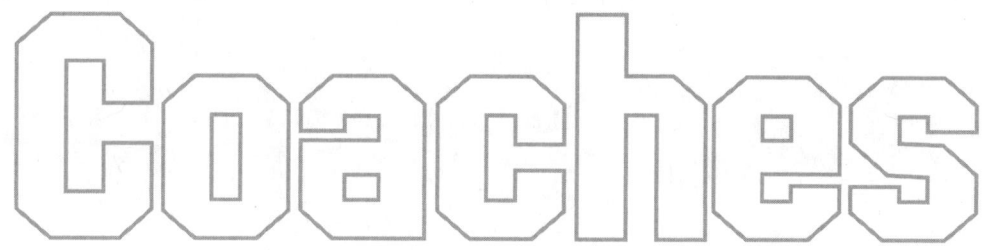

Coaches

When a coach and official lose their cool, they have only one person to blame — Each other. *themselves*

Give the coach too much rope and he will hang YOU.

If you approach every coach's question with an open mouth, you won't hear the question.

If you ever have the opportunity to visit with opposing coaches at the same time, listen politely and believe neither.

"To be honest with you coach…" Simply implies someone is probably already mad at you and that everything previously stated may not be true.

A coach's opinion is usually a minimum of facts, combined with prejudice and emotion. Approach him with that understanding and patience.

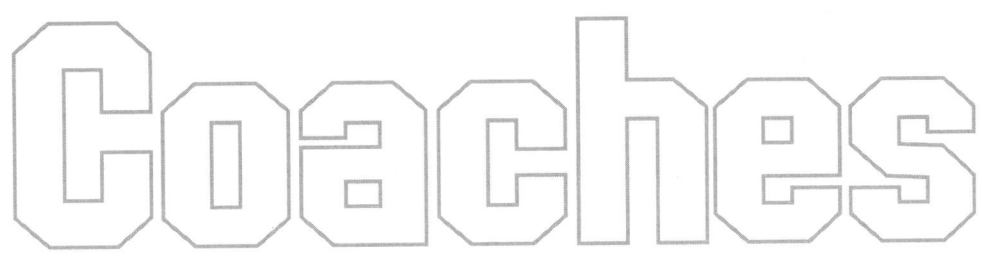

Unlike water, we boil at different degrees. If you don't have the ability to read an "oral" thermometer between you and the coach, the next time the coach may try to use a "rectal" one.

◆

When dealing with a coach, remember that discussions are an exchange of knowledge and that arguments are an exchange of ignorance. ✓

◆

When giving advice to a coach, it is best to keep it brief.

◆

A coach's anger is ¾ his lack of understanding, and the remainder is a lack of self-control. Try to find agreement on something and leave quickly.

◆

The most dangerous of all communications with a coach is the truth slightly distorted.

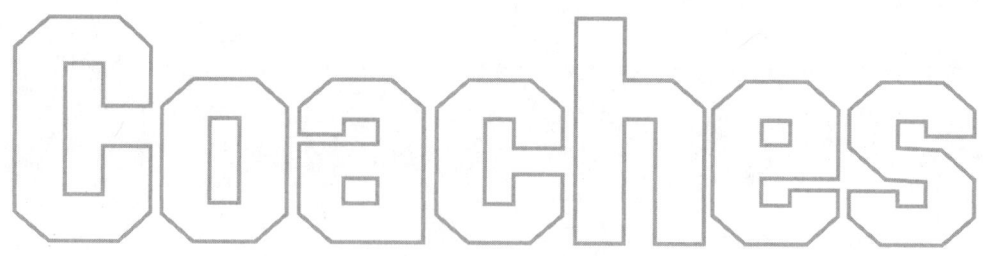

Coaches

When the coach is right and you are ducking his questions, the real problem for you is that you need a few good answers.

◆

If you don't listen to the question that the coach is asking, it is easy to give him YOUR answer.

◆

Understanding the disagreement between you and the coach is simply the short cut to a mutual understanding to disagree.

◆

A good reminder, when visiting with the coach: the goal is to EXPRESS and not to IMPRESS.

◆

When the coach is giving you "hell" on the sideline, try to envision how many fish you have seen on the wall with their mouths shut.

◆

It is easy for an official to be "popular" among coaches, but it is more difficult to be perceived as fair.

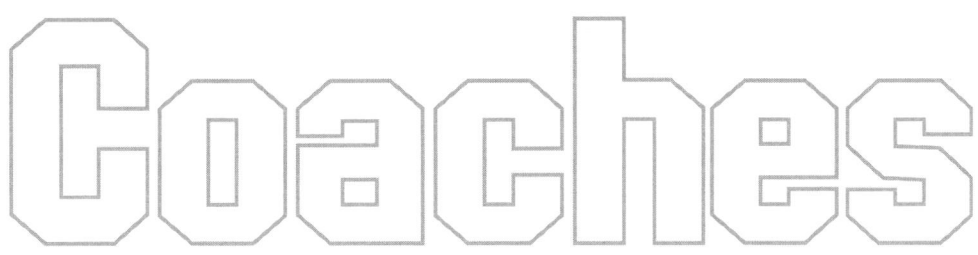

Coaches

A sense of humor appropriately timed can be the shortest distance between a coach and an official.

—◆—

There is nothing made worse than giving a coach information that he does not need.

—◆—

Show me a coach who claims to be "objective" and I'll show you a coach with illusions.

—◆—

When you feel you are being verbally attacked by a coach, don't attack back, but deflect his words and create distance.

—◆—

Mature officials have the ability to listen to almost anything from a head coach without losing their temper or self-confidence. They draw the line and penalize any time it becomes personal.

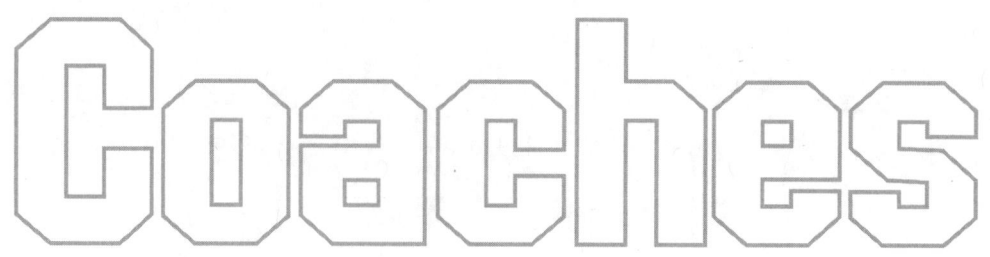

Coaches

The I.Q. and the career of the average coach pass each other when he creates a scene for himself rather than what is best for the game.

◆

One problem coaches have with officials is that they are expected to believe what we have described as the truth when the big screen is showing a "different visual" explanation of what actually happened.

◆

When a coach sincerely believes that you are selling out the integrity of the game, your officiating career will soon be bankrupt if that perception continues.

◆

When no hate is wasted between a coach and an official, it is always a lose/lose situation.

◆

It is always a good idea to be in touch with the head coach; just stay out of "reach."

Coaches

Be tactful when visiting with the coach. Know how far you can go, and stop one sentence short.

◆

The best thing to tell a coach when you have made a mistake is "Coach, I have made a mistake."

◆

Some officials try to "talk" through their game with a coach. The problem evolves when they eat more words than they speak.

◆

Sometimes the very best you can expect as a referee is agreement between you and the coach when the result of the play was not fair.

◆

You don't have to forgive a coach for being an "ass," but the best officials simply forget it.

◆

Allow a coach's illogical anger to die of neglect.

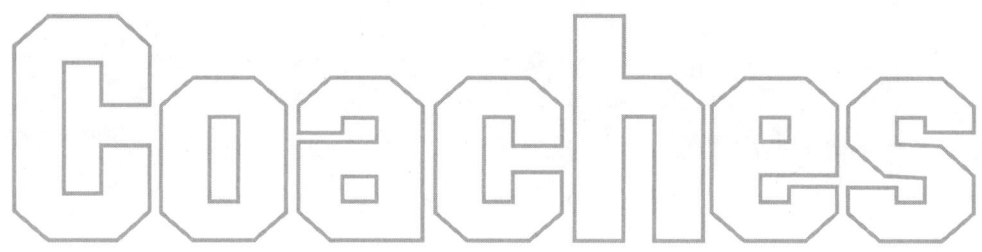

Coaches

Don't treat negative coaches with the disrespect they deserve. ✓

———◆———

As you walk towards the coach who was fired the week before, keep in mind that it is never a good idea to stay too long on the sideline with a man who has nothing to lose.

———◆———

You can't wait until you have an argument with a coach to create a positive relationship.

———◆———

The greatest danger in arguing with a coach over "Mickey Mouse" issues is that it will probably cloud the chance for handling more difficult, permanent realities of the game.

———◆———

In a difficult situation with a coach, explain the situation first and then the rule.

Coaches

My messages to coaches: Much outcry, generally little outcome.

A nagging coach is generally the simple repetition of things he wishes were true.

When the going gets tough with a coach, remember that truce is better than friction.

Some sideline officials when approaching a coach, have all the charisma of a speed bump.

When visiting with a difficult coach, speak softly and carry a big carrot.

When you are in a discussion with a coach, make sure that you keep track of when you are "pretending."

The true test of moral courage of a football official is his ability to ignore a verbal insult from a coach. (If it was personal and ignored, you just failed the test).

◆

When dealing with an irate coach, choose patience over fury.

◆

Diplomacy: the art of communicating professionally with a coach until it becomes necessary to find your flag.

◆

Some quiet coaches have a tendency on the inside to be very "outgoing."

◆

Conflicts between coaches and officials have a "natural life span." The trick is to know when to let them die.

◆

If you and the coach are "having words," it isn't necessary to use yours.

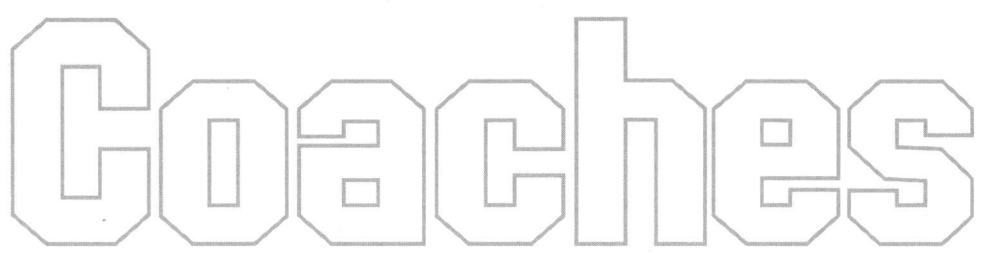

The best way to keep a coach from jumping down your throat is to keep your mouth shut. ✓

———◆———

The head coach, one hour before the game, may be a genius at football, but speaks with the I.Q. of a fifth grader — Be patient and respectful.

———◆———

The end of a conversation with a coach is never justified by meanness.

———◆———

If you believe you have won an argument with a coach, it isn't over yet.

———◆———

How to have two quick strikes when visiting with a coach: "I am not arguing with you; I am telling you."

———◆———

Coach's tip: Save yourself 15 yards by using silence as the perfect scorn.

———◆———

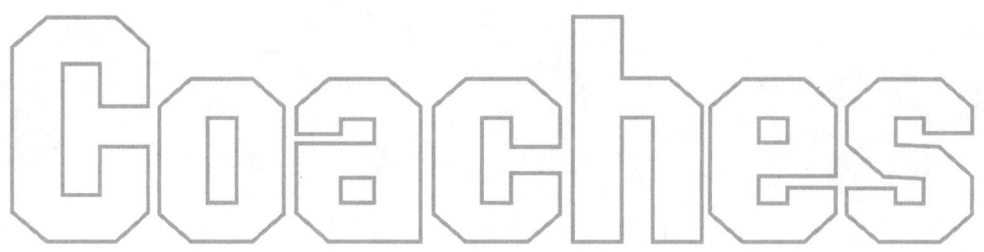

Be aware of the coach who is big enough to eat the team mascot.

◆

There are some ideas that coaches have about football rules that are so wrong that only the very intelligent official can understand.

◆

Most coaches are great Sunday through Friday, and then on "game day" some develop impeccably bad taste.

◆

Most coaches like football officials when officials are not in uniform.

◆

Some coaches' practice of deception is so constant that they begin to believe it is true.

◆

When a coach is angry, get ready for an inarticulate response.

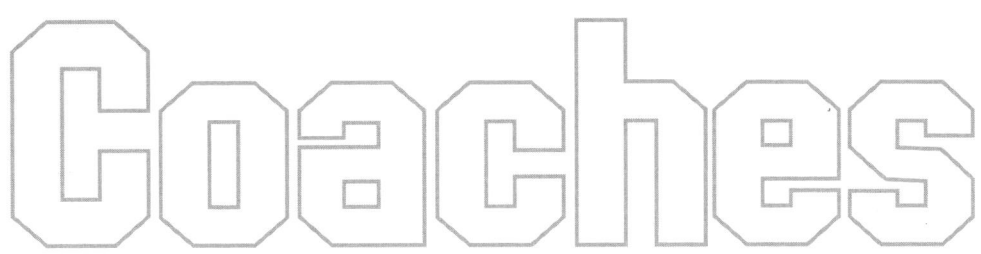

When confronted by an angry coach, the best armor is to keep out of range.

―――◆―――

The best way to deal with a coach who simply likes to argue, is to agree with him on some point and then leave.

―――◆―――

It is not uncommon when the referee meets the coach prior to the start of the game, to feel like he wants you to come and see him when you have less time.

―――◆―――

A good lesson in life to remember on the football field is that sometimes coaches are right and to respond appropriately.

―――◆―――

Don't overestimate the decency of some head coaches and most assistant coaches.

Coaches

Head coaches are the only honest hypocrites.

◆

Keep in mind that even "bad" coaches were children at one time, and their mother is probably watching the game on TV.

◆

I know a few coaches who will end up dying in their own arms.

◆

The attitude of some coaches before the game, reminds me of dead fish before they have had time to stiffen or smell.

◆

Never use one syllable to a coach when none will do.

◆

Some coaches you really have to get to know to dislike.

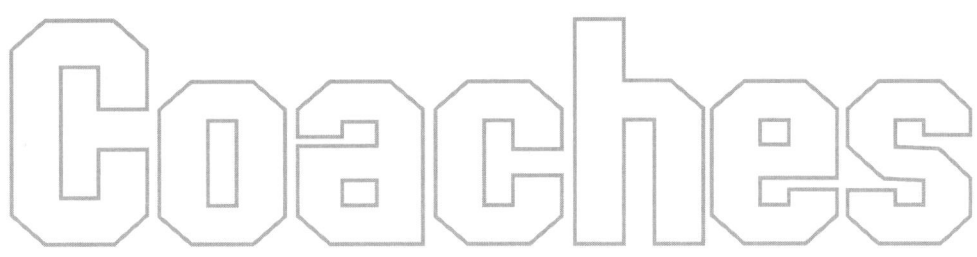

Be on the lookout for the double-talking coach who will try to carry on two contradictory conversations with you simultaneously and accept both as being right.

It is not impressive to the visiting coach when he observes how well officials appear to "obey" the home coach.

When an argument develops with a coach, don't try to win the argument, but try to agree on a concern.

Some coaches believe that in order to argue, they must be vulgar to be convincing. Too bad poor officials agree.

Have you ever noticed how some of the best known coaches say the nastiest things in the nicest ways?

Keep in mind when visiting with a coach, it is not a question as to who is right, but what is right.

◆

When a coach is kicking at you, he has only one leg to stand on.

◆

When you really want to get even with a coach, just remember if you are successful, you have reached his level.

◆

Don't offer a coach an excuse that you would not be willing to accept.

◆

Be careful when visiting with a coach that your "open mind" is not perceived as being vacant.

Section 2

Communication

The University of Oklahoma
Football Office   Room E-8   Norman, Oklahoma 73019

SOONERS

NATIONAL CHAMPIONS
1950 1974
1955 1975
1956 1985

CONFERENCE CHAMPIONS
1915 1957
1918 1958
1920 1959
1938 1962
1943 1967
1944 1968
1946 1972
1947 1973
1948 1974
1949 1975
1950 1976
1951 1977
1952 1978
1953 1979
1954 1980
1955 1984
1956 1985

ORANGE BOWL
1939
1954
1956
1958
1959
1963
1968
1976
1978
1979
1980
1981
1985
1986

SUGAR BOWL
1949
1950
1951
1972

GATOR BOWL
1947
1965

BLUEBONNET BOWL
1968
1970

FIESTA BOWL
1976
1983

SUN BOWL
1981

November 17, 1986

Mr. John Laurie
654 LaSalle
Springfield, Missouri 65807

Dear John:

I looked for you after the game but got grabbed up by the television and media people. I wanted to apologize for losing my poise -- you were right and I was wrong. But it's damn tough sometimes to try to get you guys attention to talk with you. I don't think it works just standing over there holding up a hand. But anyway, it shouldn't have happened. I'm sorry for what I said.

See you down the road.

Sincerely,

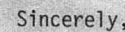

Barry Switzer
Head Football Coach

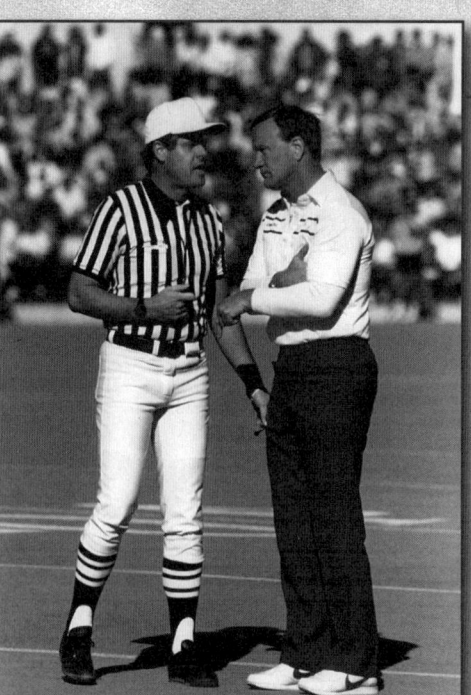

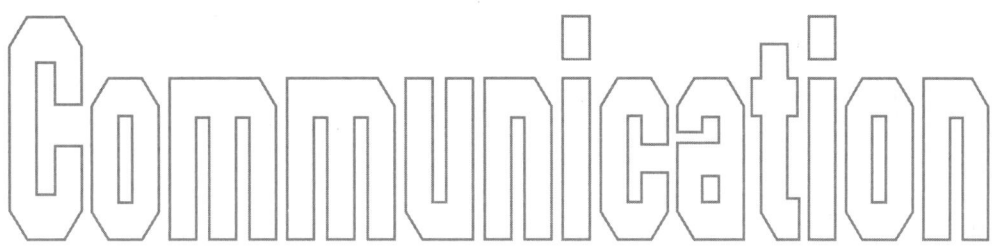

Communication

Effective communication on the field with coaches, or frankly in getting along in the world, are certainly a part of being successful at whatever we do. In this section of the book, the importance of effective communication is viewed from several perspectives.

Almost every major mistake in a football game has a halfway moment — A split second when it can be reviewed, individually and collectively by the crew, and perhaps remedied.

◆

It is a big misfortune, when talking to a coach to neither have enough tact and information to communicate well, nor enough judgment to be silent.

◆

Sometimes a little bit more information than you need can result in making the wrong decision.

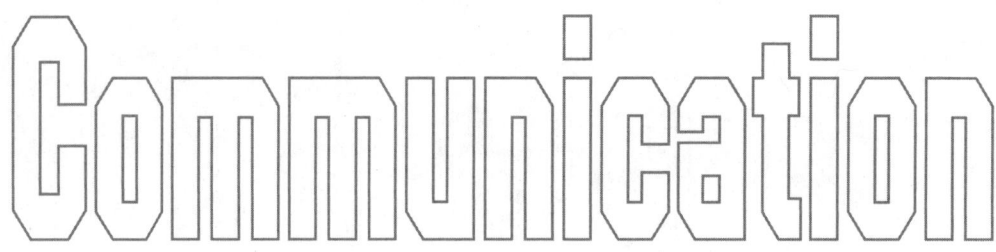

Explaining something unnecessarily to an angry coach is like adding charcoal lighter to hot coals.

◆

When the crew is trying to make a decision on a play, it is much better to not have any information than mis-information.

◆

It is much more difficult to ask the right question of an official, than to find the right answer for the wrong question.

◆

Beware of the official who can give you a definite "maybe" about what he saw.

◆

Too much information about any play will cause "loss of common sense." The key is to simply filter out unnecessary information.

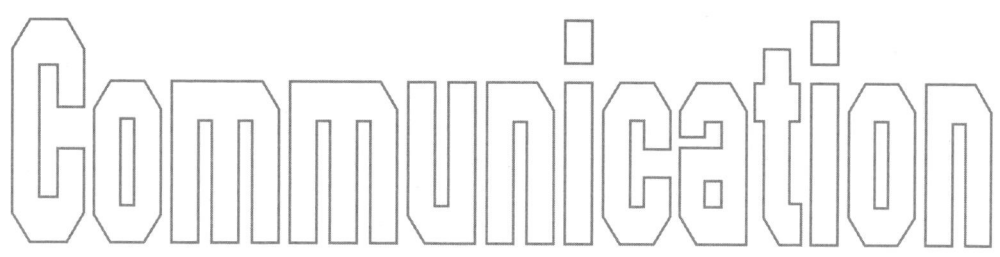

Communication

When dealing with a coach over a complicated and difficult decision, try to focus on your decision and not your reasons because from his point of view, your reasons will always be wrong.

◆

Any exaggeration that you make to a coach about a correct call weakens the strength of your statement.

◆

Some officials bring information and some officials bring communication to the referee. The big difference is that those bringing information are giving out and those communicating are getting through.

◆

Getting in a hurry to get information from your crew is the mother of mistakes.

◆

The key to a successful conversation with a coach is to agree to disagree and still carry on an appropriate conversation.

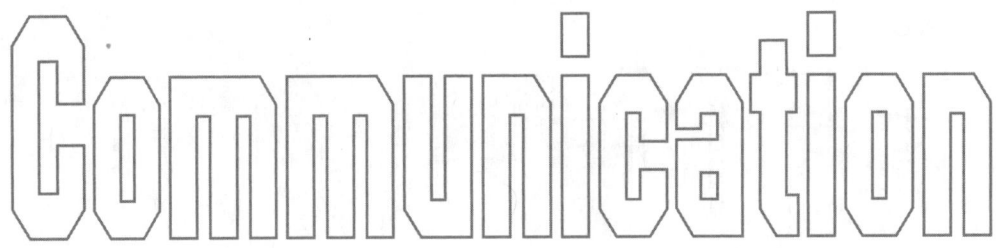

Communication

Swearing is a poor official's attempt to be emphatic.

Officiating without communication is like a bird without wings.

If it takes a lot of words to explain a situation to the coach, give it more thought and keep it shorter.

When conferring with a coach, try the sunbeam approach and simply give him a tan. Just remember that the more you condense your comments and your tone, the deeper the burn.

The next best thing to working through a difficult situation on the field is to find some humor in it. It can contribute to a funny way of being serious.

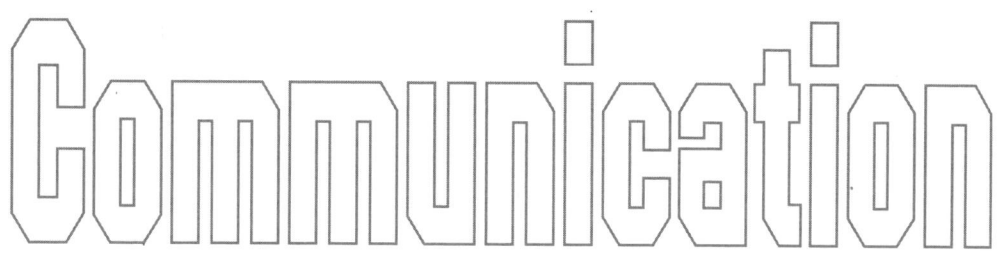

Communication

When visiting with a coach, think carefully as you are walking towards him as to what you want to say as mis-used words often generate mis-leading thoughts.

———◆———

Sometimes in order to communicate with a coach, you need to mirror his qualities: ignorance and confidence. ✓

———◆———

When a referee circles a set of options in his mind, someone in the crew needs to be aware of a wider set than his mind set.

———◆———

When in doubt, huddle — Most problems on the football field require collective solutions.

———◆———

A preconceived notion by the referee will close the door of communication and open several windows for errors.

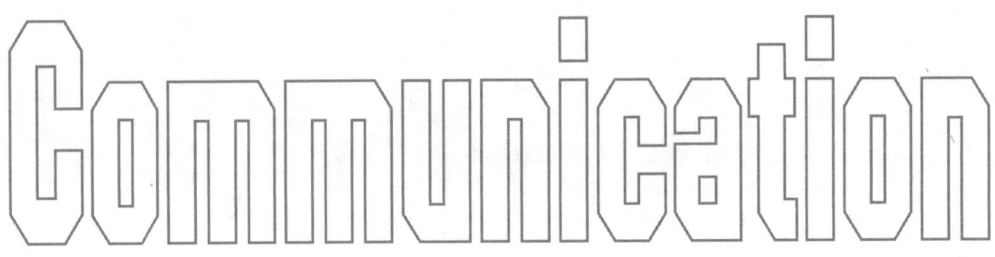

Communication

When you have key information and don't bring it to the rest of your crew, your mistake in the eyes of the crew is bigger than the one the crew is about to make.

◆

The best armor against an irate coach is to, whenever you can, stay out of his range.

◆

It is time to stop talking to a coach when he nods his head in agreement and says nothing.

◆

Problems during a football game can be resolved if properly defined with good information. Someone on the crew almost always has the missing information to solve the problem.

◆

Saying "I don't know," when you really don't know, is going to allow you to be a better official.

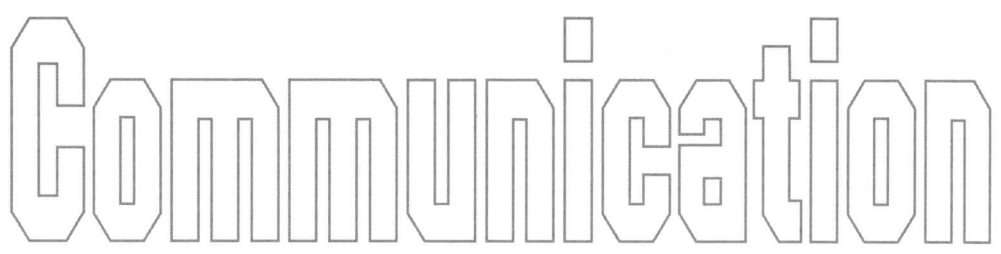

Communication

The best conversation with a coach is to say what needs to be said…Not what could be said.

◆

When dealing with coaches, remember you are not dealing with men of logic but men of emotion; men bristling with prejudice and motivated by pride and vanity.

◆

Never tell a coach, "It's not my call."

◆

If you have been to the sideline to visit with a coach about an error once, and now it is time to return to explain an inadvertent whistle, be careful what you say, and only open your mouth to change feet.

◆

On any given play, a crew will receive information from usually four to seven members. When gaining information to make a tough decision, understand the source and rationale before reacting.

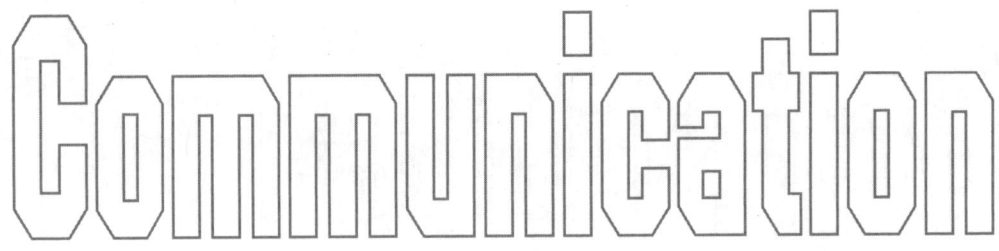

When engaged in a very difficult conversation with a coach, remember you can't get hurt by anything you don't say.

◆

When talking to a coach, generally the more you say, the less it means. (Respond with statements and avoid asking questions which make it easier to argue.)

◆

When a confrontation occurs between an official and coach, an excellent but difficult task is to try to find an area of agreement and build rather than "argue" the differences of perception.

◆

When in a heated conversation (argument) with a coach, remember it is better to be quiet and be perceived as a fool than to speak out and remove all doubt.

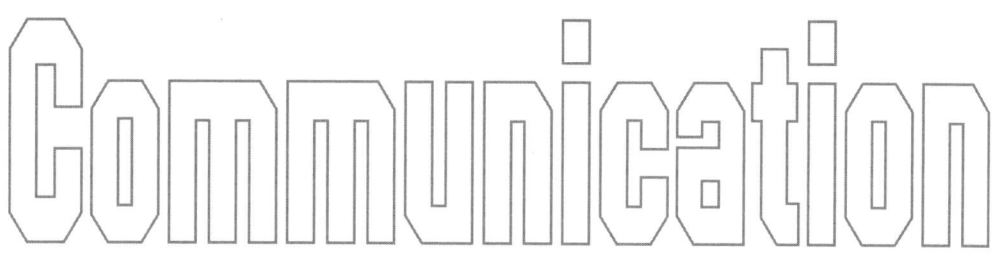

Communication

"Never murder a man who is committing suicide."
Woodrow Wilson

It is so simple to be wise. Just think of something stupid to say to a coach and then don't say it.

If the coach is ignorant of the facts, you can't win the argument. If the facts aren't in his favor, be brief, and leave.

You won't win when you are talking to a coach who is acting like a fool, because he will call you foolish in the paper the next day.

Patience with a difficult coach can be a bitter pill, but the result can leave a "sweet taste" for both the coach and the official.

Don't trust an official who gives a lot of advice, but is slow to accept suggestions from others.

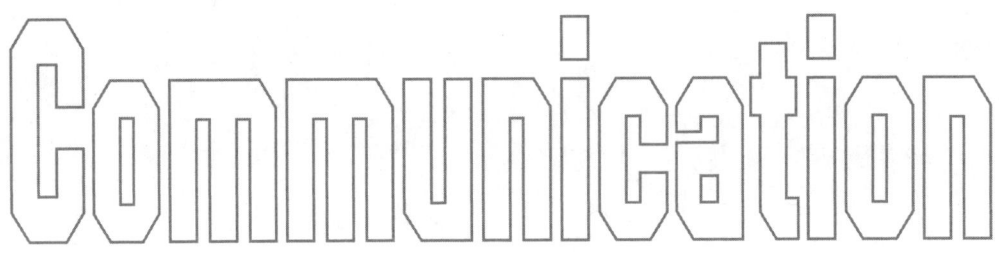

Communication

To escape the criticism from every good coach and reporter that I have ever known, do these three things: Say nothing, do nothing, and be nothing.

◆

If you are in a "tight" difficult conversation with a coach, never "cut" what you can untie.

◆

Light travels faster than sound. That is why some coaches appear brighter until you hear them speak.

◆

"Coach, we agree on everything, including the fact that we don't see eye-to-eye on what is happening on the field today."

◆

It is okay to scream at a coach…Silently.

◆

A wise official finds a way for the coach to feel like he was understood and is getting his way; when in fact, the coach was understood and the official is applying rules and reason and getting his way.

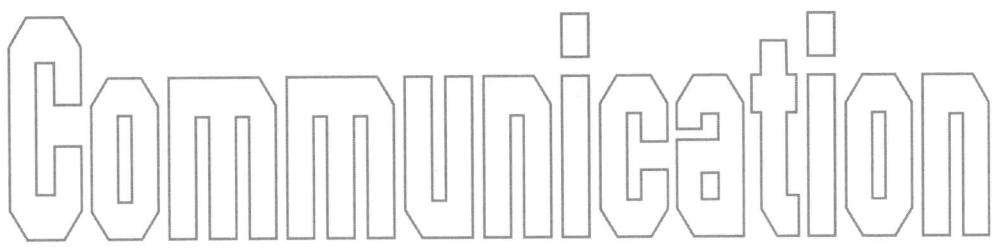

Communication

A sharp tongue with a coach can cut your throat with the conference.

---◆---

If your conversation with the coach has no way of ending professionally, do what he is trying to do and get your retaliation in first and try to leave without penalizing him.

---◆---

It is said that a circle is the longest distance to the same point — But circling the crew is the shortest way to getting the truth.

---◆---

When a crew conference is held to determine what has happened, all that some may offer is their own confusion.

---◆---

Don't condemn the judgment or question an official because their opinions differ from your own...You both may be wrong.

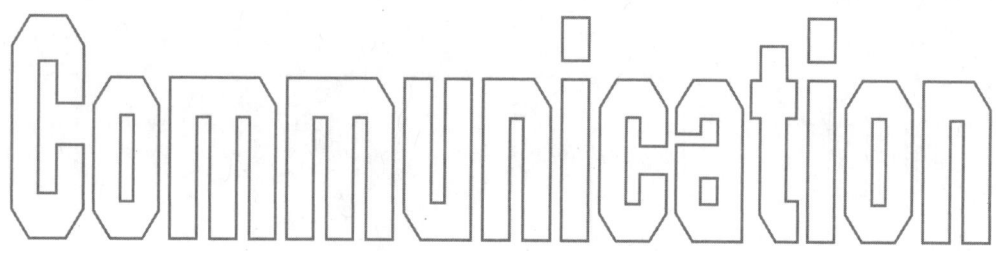

Communication

When visiting with the coach, keep in mind that effective communication is 20% what you know and 80% how you feel. Have confidence in what you are saying as that is his first impression of you BEFORE he hears what you have to say.

◆

Journalists and announcers can be tough. Never fear criticism when you are right and never ignore criticism when you are wrong. ✓

Attack the behavior not the character of the person.

◆

The best way to effectively reprimand a member of your crew is to fit the reprimand to the official's own self-image. ✓

◆

When huddling with the crew, remember that information can be pretty thin stuff unless there is some experience mixed in.

◆

The best way to solve the most complicated situations that occur on the field is to ask the right questions.

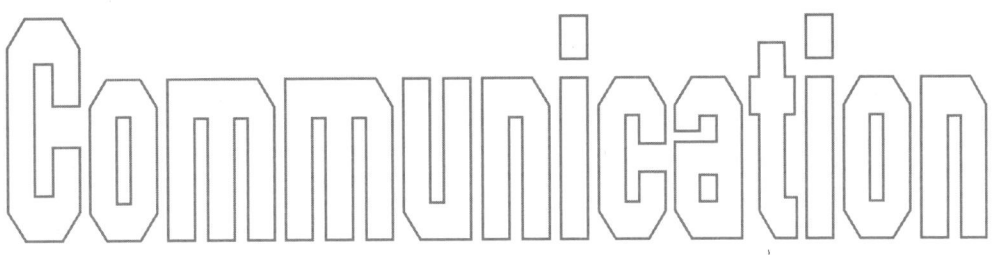

Communication

When an official comes to the referee and says "I may be wrong, but…" Just back off and believe that it ain't very good information.

———◆———

It is difficult to solve the problem on the field when you haven't figured out that a problem exists.

———◆———

Try this one on a coach: "That is the most unheard of football rule I have ever heard."

———◆———

Some situations can become so emotional and confusing on the field, if you are not somewhat frustrated and confused by the information you have received, you simply do not understand the problem.

———◆———

Mis-used words = mis-understood thoughts, which = mistakes and ill feelings.

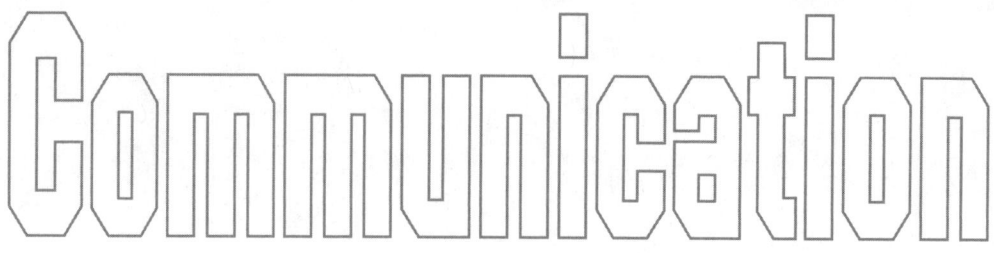

There are two sides to the thinnest pancake as there are two sides of the football field to communicate with during the game.

The official who gets in trouble most often with a coach has difficulty keeping quiet when he has nothing to say.

If the referee assembles his crew to discuss a key play in the game and his comment begins, "I don't want any half-truths unless they are completely accurate…" Try to get on a new crew.

Don't answer a coach's question with a lecture.

Beware of officials who love to ask questions, but are never open to answers.

In the post-game discussion, remember several excuses are less convincing than one.

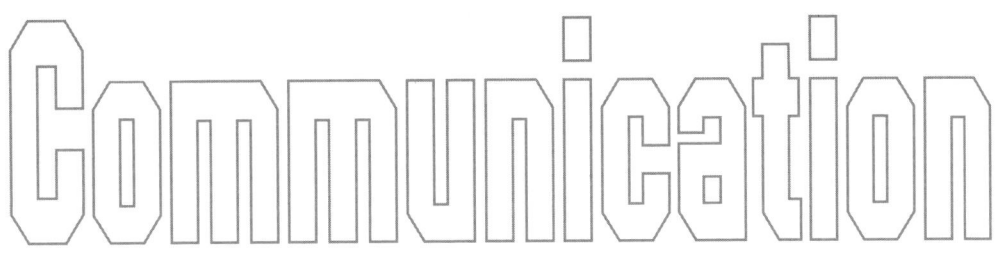

When conversing with a coach and thought is lacking, don't allow words to show up.

―――♦―――

Interesting that officials who know the least about football, talk the most; and those who know the game, say little.

―――♦―――

To make sense out of non-sense, make sure your two cents is of value to the solution.

―――♦―――

It is a good idea not to express yourself to a coach or the media more clearly than you can think.

―――♦―――

Never put the blame on another crew member when talking to the coach, if the issue is your own stupidity.

―――♦―――

Be alert for press conferences. Never underestimate the power of very stupid people in large groups.

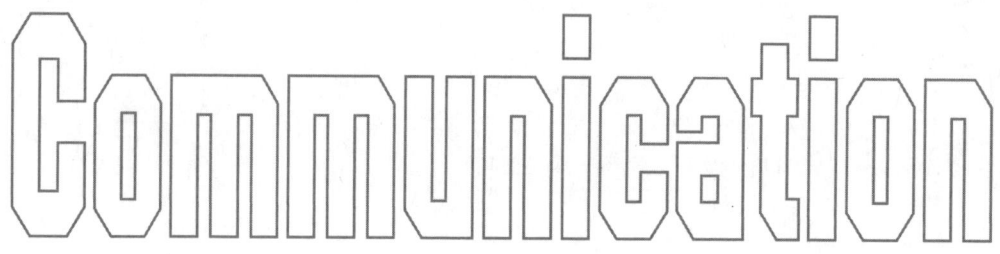

When you add to the truth of a situation when explaining something to a coach, you subtract from it as well as lose integrity.

◆

If you listen too carefully to an irate coach, you will hear more than you need or want to hear.

◆

The first rule in communicating with a coach is to be a good listener.

◆

If you want to be known as a "poor communicator" with coaches, always agree with them.

◆

When dealing with a coach, there is a degree of tolerance and a narrow moment in time which borders on insult. The trick is to first try to defuse the issue if possible and, then of course, penalize.

◆

Sometimes the only way to communicate with an irate coach is to be obscure, as clearly as possible.

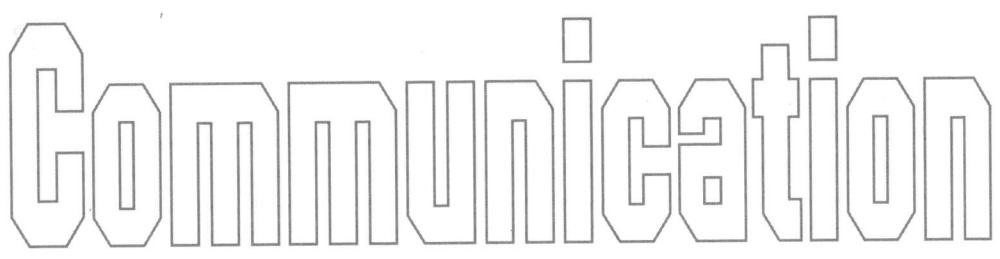

Communication

When a coach is waving at you that he would like for you to come to him for a "chat" — Listen, but try to get a little closer apart.

The quickest and easiest discussion with a coach over a difficult situation is not always the best; sometimes the longest distance between two points of view is a "short cut."

It does not take a brave dog to bark at the bones of a lion, nor an official or coach to talk about some parts of the game to the press.

The best way of handling an emotional argument with a coach is to let it go on with simply no response.

If you have fear of making the coach mad, your highest result of conversation will be reaching the lowest form of respect and human achievement in official/coach communication.

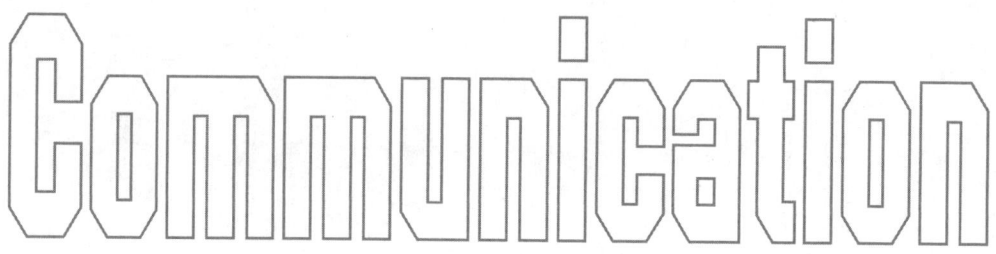

Communication

Coaches and officials who are successful listen first; losers just wait for their turn to talk.

◆

If your explanation to a coach is too weak to explain, reconsider what you are trying to accomplish.

◆

The general perception of a coach/official conversation is: "He does not hear what I say, and I don't say what he wants to hear."

◆

What did the coach say to you while you were being chewed out? "Let's just say he was a toothache of a coach."

◆

When a coach is really yelling his head off at you, don't turn and look, but it might be improving his appearance.

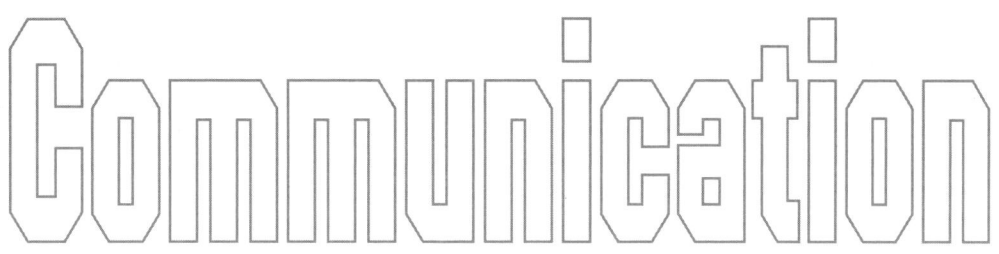

There is a very special exact psychological moment when an official knows it is best to say nothing to anger a coach.

◆

A speech or lecture to a coach is not nearly as effective as silence.

◆

My rank order responses to an angry coach: Listen, silence, smile politely, leave, if necessary, explain/respond and try to reach agreement, and not staying for the last word.

◆

Simple rule: If you have trouble communicating with a coach…Don't. Just listen and leave.

◆

Well-timed silence is "golden" when no response to an angry coach is appropriate.

◆

Don't let your enthusiasm show gray before your hair.

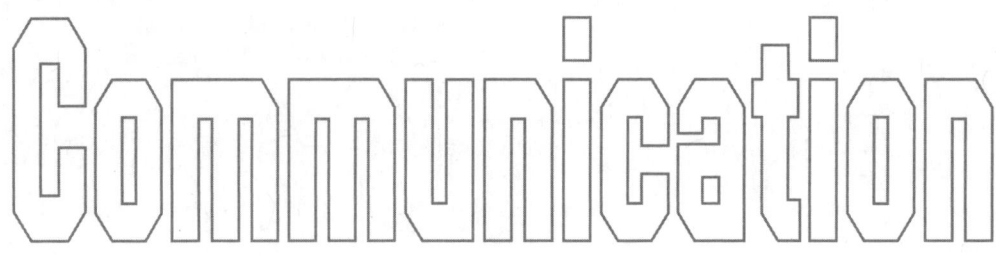

Communication

If some officials are going to "practice what they preach," they are going to need a few overtimes to get the job done. An argument between a coach and an official is the longest distance between two points of view.

Beware of the crew member who brings gossip from other crews, as he is also your leak.

Flashes of silence can keep an irate coach from exploding.

"Tact" is to apply the rules of the game to an irate coach and allow him to believe he still knows more about the game than you.

All talk and no show is like a garden full of weeds.

Crew rumors are deadly tales with stingers.

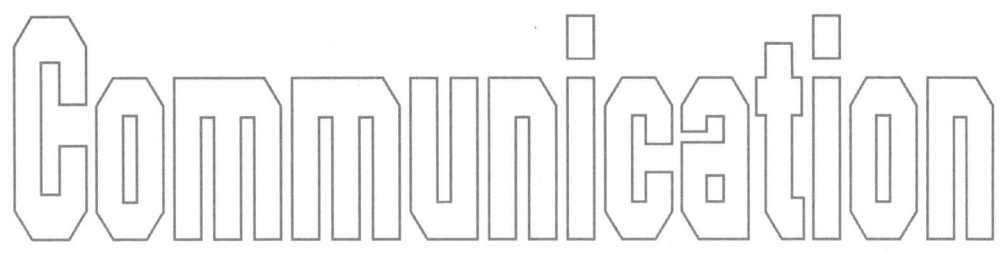

If you cannot think of nice things to say about your crew, check the mirror before you put on your uniform.

♦

You can't see "eye to eye" with a coach, player or crew member if you look down upon them.

♦

Sometimes the best "last word" to a coach is an apology.

♦

When in a confrontation with a coach, it is good to remember that there is a slim margin between keeping your chin up and sticking your neck out.

♦

Simple solutions to difficult situations may not always be right, but it is the best place to start.

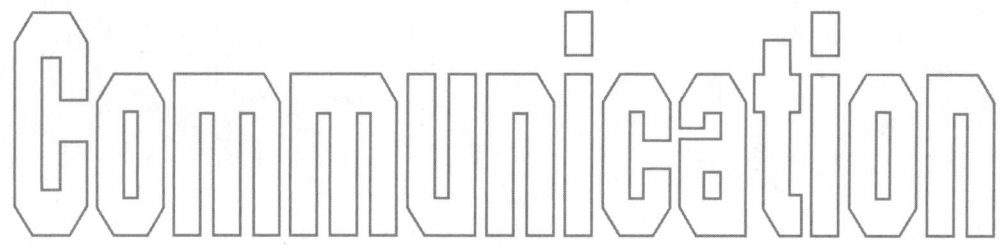

Communication

Most of the time the official and coach are not going to change their minds about a situation. Therefore, try to change the subject, reach agreement, and return to your position.

◆

An official's judgment is no better than the information he receives.

◆

The start of a good conversation, when a coach wants to visit, is first silence and then listen. It may or may not be necessary that you say anything.

◆

If a coach is a mental midget with the I.Q. of a rock, look him in the eye, listen patiently for 5 seconds, take two steps backward and then return to your position.

◆

Trying to "talk sense" to a coach acting like a fool will only result in a quote on the sports page by the coach the next day describing how you "acted like a fool."

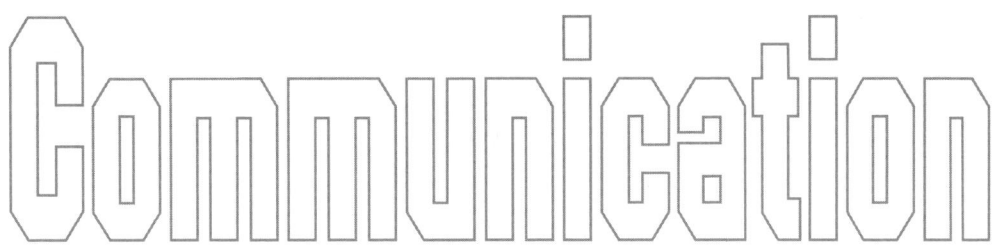

Communication

Never be rude to a coach who is always unintentionally rude.

―――◆―――

A coach's idea of "good communication" is keeping you on the sideline until he convinces you he was right!

―――◆―――

The longer the argument between an official and a coach, the greater the chance that you both are wrong.

―――◆―――

Visible, emotional speculation by a coach is best ignored unless it becomes "personal" or excessive.

―――◆―――

If you have trouble communicating with your crew, shut up.

Great officials, great friends — left to right: Mike Liner, Lubbock, TX; Brad Horchem, Shawnee, KS; Phil Laurie, Topeka, KS; John Laurie, Overland Park, KS; Richard Whittenburg, Lubbock, TX; John Robinson, Bountiful, UT; Tim Crowley, Austin, TX. (Oklahoma @ Nebraska)

Section 3

Confidence

CONFIDENCE: (Len Williams/John Laurie) Confidence can be reinforced through constant and appropriate communication on the field throughout the game.

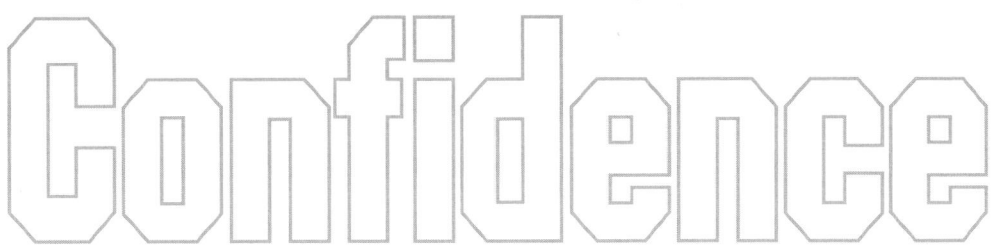

Confidence

I have never met a good sports official (again, actually any successful person) who did not display excellent confidence in himself, or what he did for a living. In sports officiating, this quality may be magnified somewhat because of the "exposure" through the media to large numbers of people. But regardless, lack of confidence plays a tremendous role in how we live and how we are accepted in the various roles we play in our lives.

> You must have the confidence you are superior to the circumstance to get through the tough ones.

◆

> When coaches and officials are the "least sure," they exaggerate the most.

◆

> When a difficult situation develops that you are not prepared for, two thoughts will pass through your mind: "This is a chance to screw this up," or "this is a chance to step up and do my best." Choose the right approach.

◆

> The best officials gain confidence from the experience of a mistake; — Poor officials crumble.

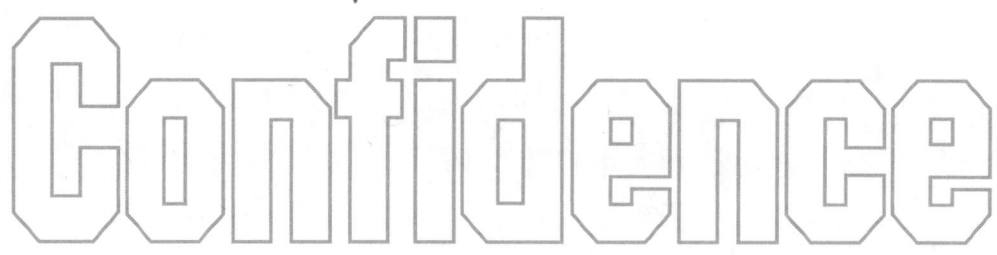

Confidence

Every crisis on the football field requires an adjustment and test of your self-esteem.

―◆―

Nothing is more destined to create deep-seated stress in officials than the false assumption that a game should be free of anxieties.

―◆―

The No. 1 back judge in the conference wants the big play in the game to come to him — No. 7 ranked is saying "I hope the hell it goes to the other side of the field."

―◆―

The barrier to successful officiating is mostly in doubting your ability.

―◆―

You can bend so far backward working with a weak official or out of control coach, that you end up burying your career directly behind you in a pile of lack of confidence.

Authority is derived by purchasing a striped shirt. Respect is earned by what is inside the shirt. ✓

---◆---

Difficult games and situations in officiating are inevitable; remaining positive is optional.

---◆---

The real test of character in an official is how he handles himself and the situation after he makes a mistake.

---◆---

A referee first inspires his crew to have confidence in him, and then he inspires the crew to have confidence in themselves. ✓

---◆---

In a football game you can learn more about yourself in ten minutes of agony than in ten games of content.

---◆---

When the pressure of a difficult situation is about to get to you — Find your temper before you lose it.

It takes more courage to act than to react.

◆

If confidence turns to conceit, you are on your way down.

◆

A nice uniform and no courage simply means there is less here than meets the eye.

◆

If your conscience "hurts" when everyone else thinks you did a great job, learn from the experience.

◆

The first step toward becoming a better official is to simply be who you are.

◆

It is okay to have a little fear before the game. If used appropriately it can take you a little closer to courage.

◆

Best crew: "They bring out the best in me."

One crew member having the courage to make the tough call is a majority.

———◆———

An official's sense of humor is very important. It is his ability to put himself in the stands as a fan and laugh at his own mistakes.

———◆———

Self-confidence is the very first step you take to become a good official.

———◆———

The most confident officials do not need to return to their "finest hour" of officiating in conversation.

———◆———

The greater an official's confidence in himself, the greater the capacity to becoming a successful official.

———◆———

The most important ingredient to become a very good official inside your uniform is your attitude.

An official with "character" does not need "extra" motivation to work a great game.

◆

Experience gives you the opportunity to officiate the "big game." Confidence allows you to do it.

◆

Before the first kick-off, self-confidence is the first requisite to officiating a great game.

◆

Every new adjustment, every change in the rules, mechanics, new crew members, difficult schedule, is a crisis in self esteem.

◆

If you want to understand what motivates you, don't look in this book or any other. Look "inside", it's not in a book.

◆

There is a big difference in wanting to become a major college official and willing to become one. ✓

Well-placed, earned confidence is the best motivator for a crew or crew member.

◆

All officials need to be "disciplined" from time to time, but the most effective and lasting is self-discipline.

◆

For some officials getting out of bed on Saturday morning is an act of false confidence.

◆

Don't depend on another official or a high-profile game for you to do your best, as it is not up to anyone else.

◆

If you think being part of a great crew is contagious, then you are a part of a great crew.

◆

An experienced official's conscience does not get its guidance from a coach or a self-centered crew member.

Confidence

Don't let nonsense keep common sense from your focus.

◆

The greater your confidence, the greater your capacity to improve. ✓

◆

Conceit is telling; — Confidence is doing.

◆

Some officials think that the opposite of officiating a good game is to officiate a bad game. Actually indifference is a greater contrast.

◆

A dependable and consistent official will always be more successful than a clever one.

◆

Progress will occur if you become dissatisfied, but not discouraged.

A confident official who "grows" into conceit becomes a smaller person.

◆

Replicating good officiating is always a good plan, but don't be a carbon copy. Make your own impression.

Section 4

"Good" Officials

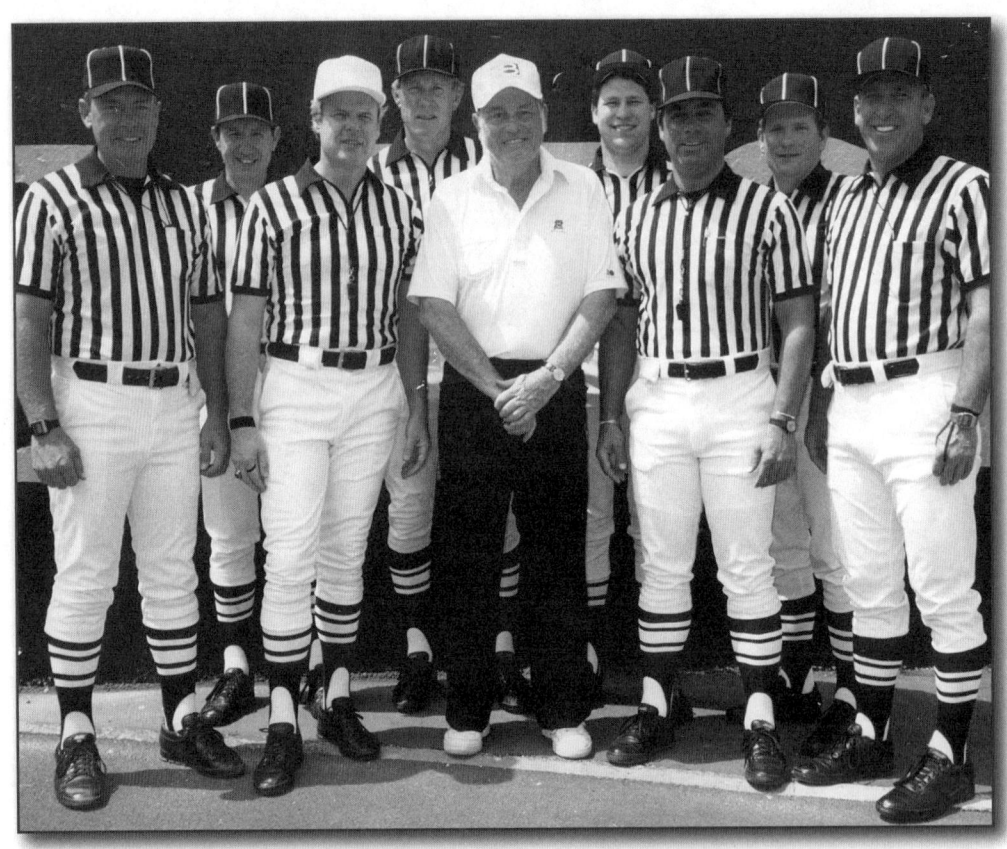

The Missouri crew 1989 — the most gifted crew that I had the opportunity to work with in college football. Left to right: Butch Clark, Terry Turlington, John Laurie, *J.C. Leimbach, *Bruce Finlayson (supervisor), *Mark Hitner, *George Hayward, *Mike Weir, *Mike Borgard. (*Crew members who worked in the NFL)

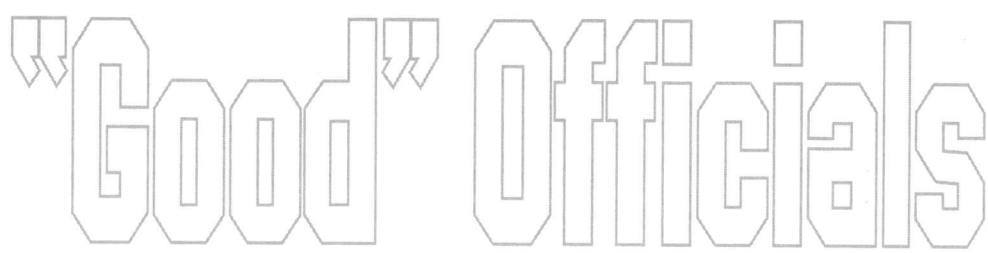

"Good" Officials

This section is designed to assist "good" officials, or those aspiring to be "better" officials, with some tips that have worked for many successful officials over the past 40 years. You will also note that none of this is really "magic" but simply outlining some "common sense" things that also apply to our daily routines.

    Some officials hesitate and make mistakes because they feel inferior. The best ones are busy making mistakes and becoming superior officials. ✓

---◆---

    The closest to a "perfectly officiated game" is not when there is nothing else to add, but when there is nothing left to take away. ✓

---◆---

    The best officials make the most difficult games appear the easiest to officiate.

---◆---

    The best officials return to their "game" quickly after a mistake. The greatest actually see it coming and prevent it. ✓

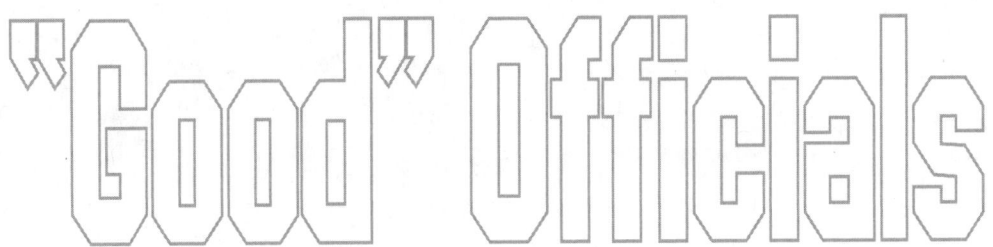

"Good" Officials

Experienced officials have the ability to discover alternatives in difficult situations.

◆

The best officials simply deal with the 10% they can NOT control, and react appropriately to the other 90%.

◆

The most successful officials have the capacity to move from a mistake to the next play without any loss of enthusiasm.

◆

The very best officials know what to overlook.

◆

The very best officials only see what they are prepared to see — That is an advantage and separates them from average.

◆

A good official sees as much as he should — But not as much as he can.

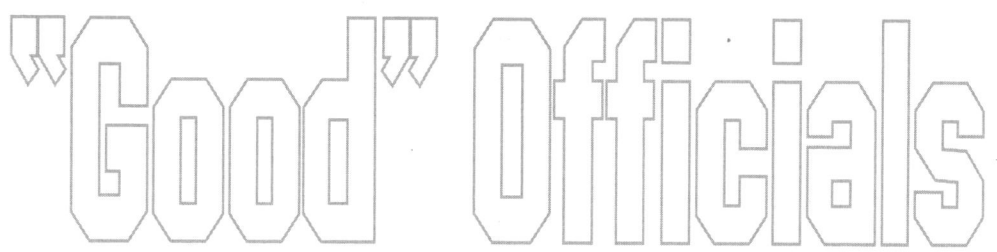

Humility is important, but the most respected officials have a good personality.

In a football game demonstrating the ability to not be distracted by things you can not change is a sign of maturity.

The true test of a great official is what level of emotion upsets him, and then how he recovers.

The most mature officials expect the unexpected.

The very best officials don't even pretend to know what many insecure officials are sure of.

Good officials are distressed by the limitations of their ability, not because the supervisor does not recognize their ability.

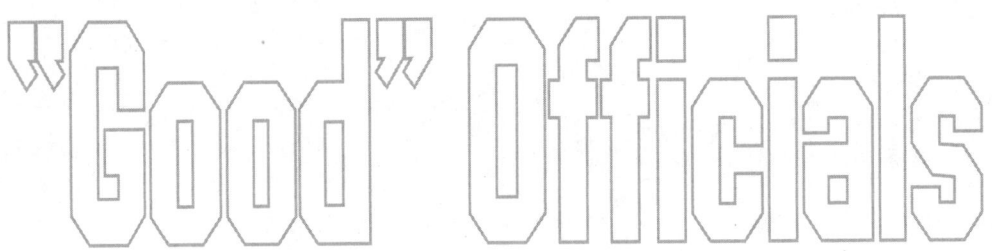

"Good" Officials

The most experienced officials have the ability to turn a train wreck on the field into a "no advantage" situation.

◆

Why is it that all officials have problems in a football game, but the very best ones seem to avoid emergencies and crises?

◆

When you reach the top, the next step is four times more difficult than the previous step it took to get there.

◆

The best officials have that extra–special drive to exceed expectations.

◆

Most officials know what is best to do. The great ones know how best to do it.

◆

Good officials recognize the problem on the field before it becomes an emergency.

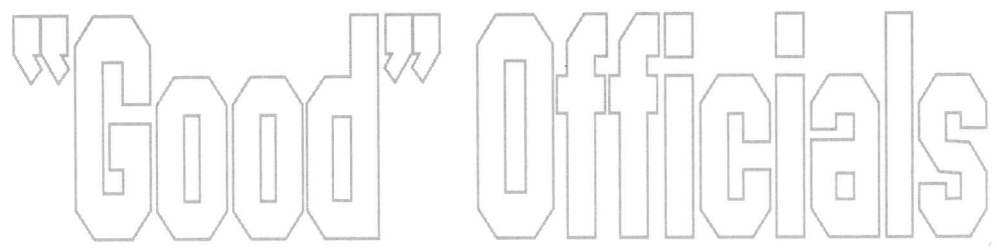

The best crews simply find ways of doing the common routine parts of a football game better than anyone else.

◆

Great officials have a way of finding creative ways to use common sense.

◆

The best officials don't let their wheels show.

◆

The qualities that an official keeps hidden determine his integrity on the field and with his crew off the field. Great officials don't hide their weaknesses; they simply find ways to reduce or eliminate them.

◆

The true test of the character of the best officials is not how they act after officiating a near-perfect game, but how they respond to a mistake during a game when it was their responsibility.

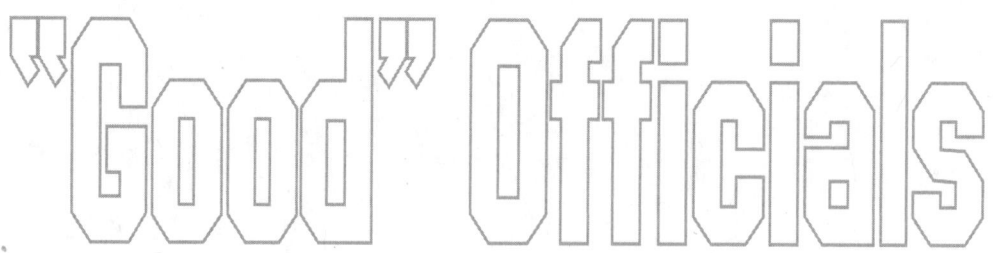

"Good" Officials

The real test for the character of a great official is manifested in the great moments of great games, but it is made possible because of successful processing of the small moments.

◆

The best officials don't anticipate the play, but they understand the consequences of what players are trying to do.

◆

The best officials have the ability to conceal their ability.

◆

Wise officials learn many things from a poorly officiated game.

◆

There comes a critical point in some very key games from time to time in your career, where without a moment of courage to step up and make the call, you miss the opportunity to be an exceptional official.

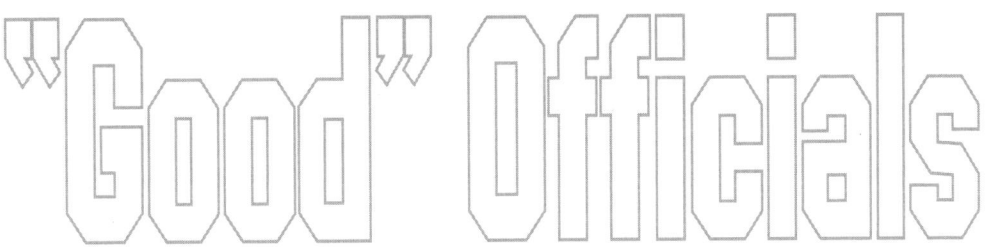

"Good" Officials

The best officials are like a 10-speed bike. They seem to have "gears" that they never need to use.

———◆———

A well-played, well-officiated football game has a flow and feel to it not unlike riding a horse in the direction it wants to go.

———◆———

The very best officials when the game really gets tough, hang on after others let go — They simply do k~~n~~ow not know how to give up!

———◆———

The best officials show their professionalism by working as hard (usually more difficult) in the last place game (toilet bowl) as the championship game.

———◆———

Generally the most silent officials are the most confident in their abilities.

———◆———

First, deserve to be the best official, and then desire to be the best.

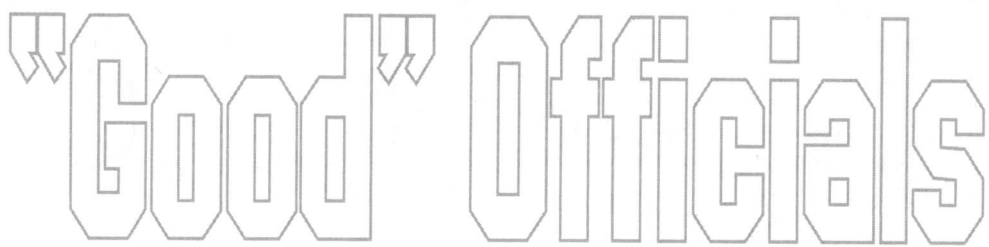

The better official you are, the more you still need to learn.

◆

The greatest success in officiating is the self-acceptance that you have done a good job.

◆

The best officials love their sport. They don't officiate because of someone else. They love the game and satisfaction of doing a good job.

◆

The ability to stay focused throughout the game is the bridge between goals and accomplishments.

◆

Good officials can take a lot of criticism, but it is also nice to get some "unqualified" praise.

◆

The best officials all have these two qualities: they must hear and be deaf, and they must see and be blind. (at the right times.)

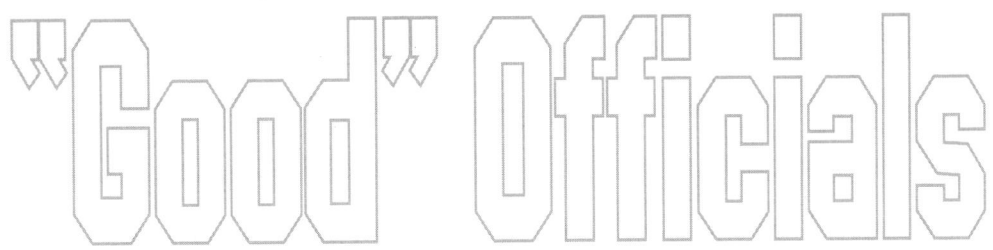

"Good" Officials

Young officials should always respect elder officials until it is difficult to find one.

——◆——

The best officials are the most calm during the biggest situations in the game. It is not uncommon for the same officials to let little things upset them during the unimportant times of the game.

——◆——

It is difficult to keep a "committed" official from succeeding.

——◆——

The fewer excuses you make, the more convincing others are of your abilities.

——◆——

The greater the official, the more acceptable his modesty becomes to others. When the coach wants a "long talk" with you, take the "long walk" to the sideline and be prepared for a "long listen" or a short career.

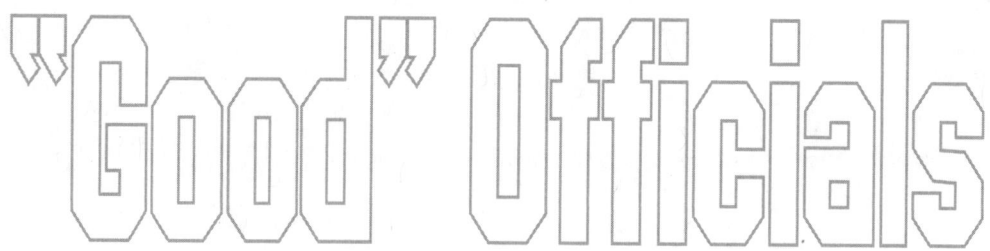

"Good" Officials

A wise official can change his mind when appropriate; a foolish one never will.

◆

Good officials can look themselves in the mirror and say that their errors were of judgment and not of rule interpretations or intent.

◆

The more that you can admit it when you have made a mistake, the more remarkable and respected you become.

◆

To establish yourself as a good official, appear established. Nothing succeeds as quickly as the appearance of success.

◆

Good officials are so focused during the biggest and most stressful games that they seem to flow with each play and simply enjoy the game.

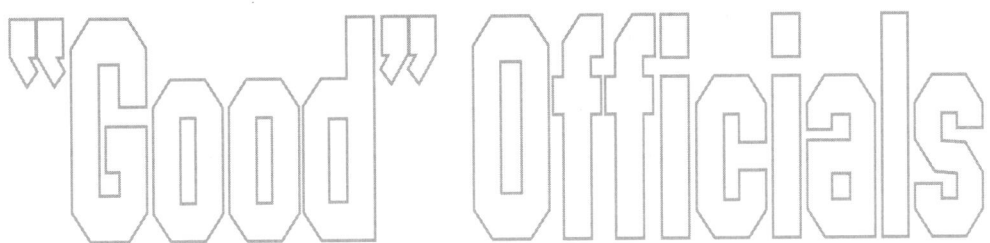

"Good" Officials

The best officials set their own quotas, and then regularly exceed them.

―◆―

The best officials are easily satisfied with the very best.

―◆―

Good officials look at difficult situations and solve them. Poor officials do their best to avoid taking any action.

―◆―

If you are looking for one word to describe a good football official, decisiveness is a good choice.

―◆―

The clear line between a good official and a great official is in that moment when a decisive quick decision is needed. The good ones think and the great ones act.

―◆―

Good officials do not need to look or act cool.

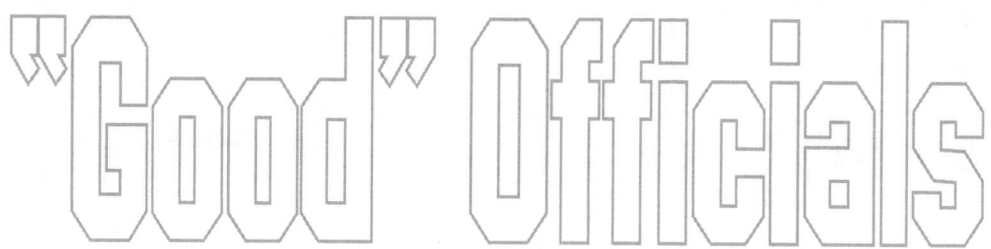

An experienced official finds ways to replicate successful situations and games.

◆

When serious mistakes are about to be made, an experienced official figures out how to avoid them.

◆

Officiating is not about being nice, but about being right, strong and professional.

◆

If a player, coach or another official can show you that you have made a wrong decision, make it a win/win situation for you and the game.

◆

The best officials in the heat of the moment are like a campfire, when things get stirred up, they shine even brighter.

◆

Good officials do what they can, the best officials do what must be done.

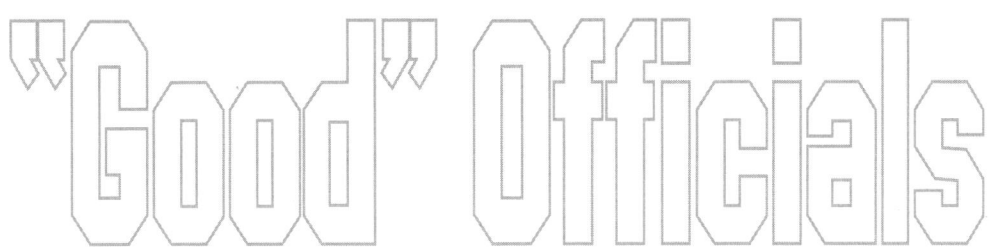

"Good" Officials

Novice officials react to what has happened; experienced officials prepare to react to what might happen.

◆

Good judgment is more than skill. It is based on good information and some innate quality far beyond the separation of what is fact and what is fiction, which good officials either have or acquire.

◆

The best officials are modest which brings a form of pride that is difficult for other officials and coaches to offend.

◆

Wise officials know when they don't know the rule or what to do. They then figure out an appropriate response to the situation. Poor officials simply guess.

◆

The very best officials have been failures from time to time.

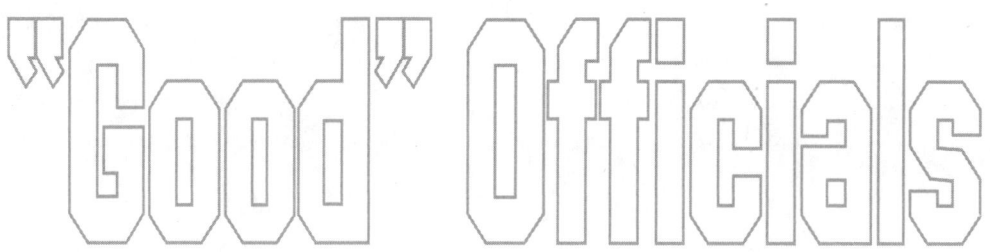
"Good" Officials

One word can summarize the best crew for all kinds of games — Flexibility.

◆

Mediocre officials see no one better than themselves. Talented officials recognize those at the very top of their game.

◆

Good officials do the difficult stuff with ease. The best officials do the impossible stuff and work through difficulty.

◆

The best crews are motivated and driven by the desire to achieve — Not to be better than other crews.

◆

When the "play of the game" arises, the best officials arise to the occasion.

◆

Every official has fear; — The best officials resist and master it.

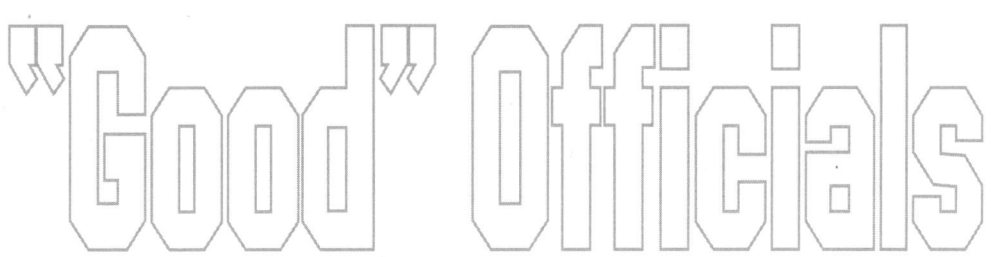

"Good" Officials

Everyone can become frightened during the emotional part of a football game. The best officials wait until after the game to check this emotion.

◆

Maturity is making a mistake and then becoming a better official.

◆

The real knowledge of a football official is to know the extent of his ignorance of the rules and simply not confuse his ignorance with the rule book.

◆

Successful officials don't wait for success to come to them — They seek it.

◆

A good official is nothing more than a bad official with applied talent.

◆

A retentive memory is a good thing for understanding football rules, but the ability to forget and forgive is the true token of a great official.

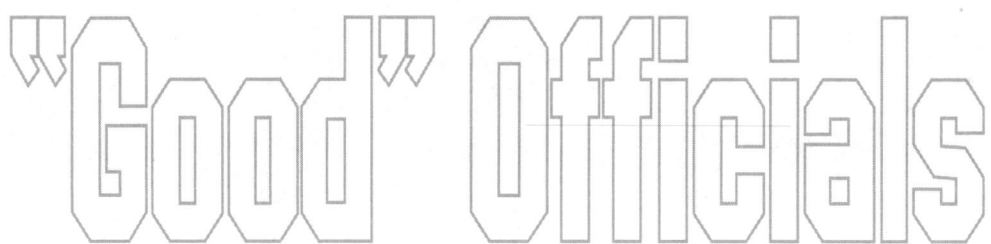

"Good" Officials

Superior officials always believe they can be better.

◆

Big-time officials don't belittle.

◆

The best officials do more than what others think wise to achieve excellence.

◆

If you hold your standard of excellence higher than anyone else has for you, you will be successful.

◆

If as an official you are consistently successful, what you have repeated on the field is not a one-time act, but a good habit.

◆

The best officials are the "talented" ones who simply do their homework.

◆

Officials at the top of their game do "whatever it takes" to work a good game. Others do what they can.

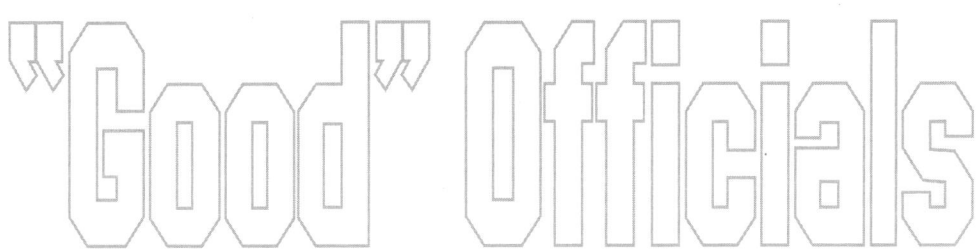

Successful officiating is repetitive: game-like practice, game-like situations, sweat, achieve, shower and then repeat.

◆

The difference between being a mediocre and high-achieving official is simply enthusiasm.

◆

The possibility of failure is never even a remote possibility for the most successful crews.

◆

Weak officials give in to misfortune; whereas, good officials rise above it.

◆

Sometimes during a football game doing your best is not enough — You must do what is necessary.

◆

Successful officials never fail because they turn their failures into a positive experience and improve.

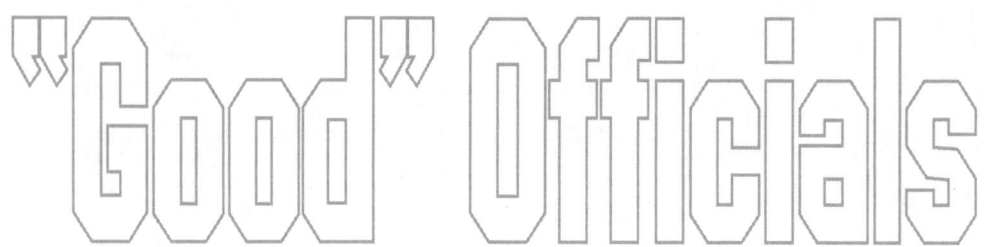

Every good official works through failure on the way to the top of their game.

◆

The use of consistent common sense will get you further in officiating than following every word written in the rule book.

◆

Behind every successful official there are some unsuccessful games, that are an important part of the finished product.

◆

It takes many seasons of excellence to develop the maturity to be known as a great official.

◆

The inexperienced official hops from situation to situation. The experienced official finds a "flow" to the game.

◆

The best officials have already given a lot of thought to sudden decisions to be made on the field.

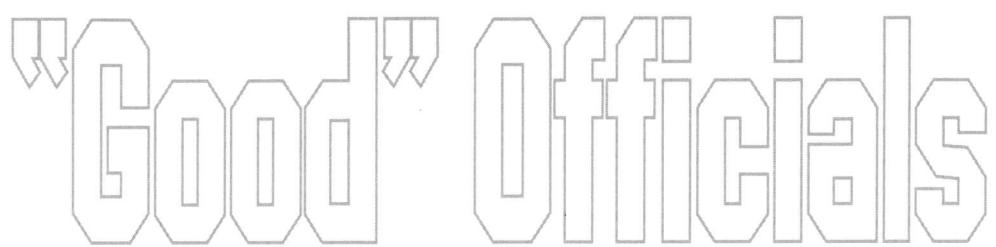

"Good" Officials

Weather or not, the best officials don't let it be a negative factor in officiating a great game.

◆

The best games are officiated by those who understand what should not be penalized, not what could be penalized.

◆

You don't become the best official at your position until you recognize that you are no longer indispensable.

◆

Secure officials are the most humble.

◆

The difference between a good and great official is little enough, but that little makes the difference.

◆

Good officials find a way; indifferent officials find an excuse.

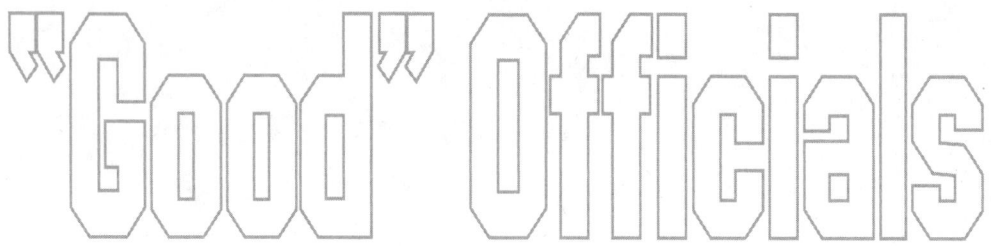

"Good" Officials

The bigger the official, the less he is aware of his size.

◆

Winners find a way of associating with winners.

◆

Past experiences are simply a guide to prevention of situations that may be similar in the future. The best officials are able to take a single experience and broaden their understanding and have a "broader" set of experiences.

◆

When a tight situation is 50-50 with no clear decision-through common sense, the good crews will get it right 90% of the time and poor crews, maybe 10% of the time.

◆

The best officials don't leave success to chance.

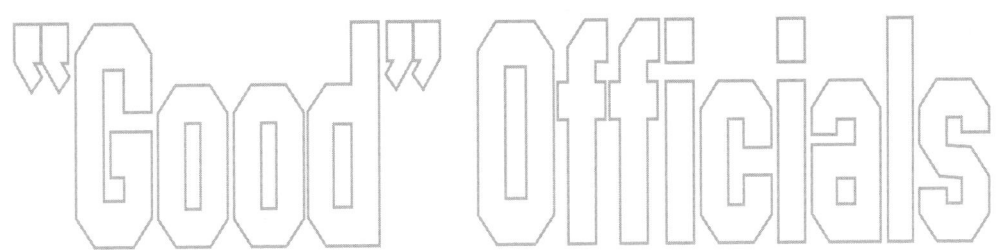

"Good" Officials

Good officials correct errors before they become mistakes.

◆

One of the differences between a good official and poor official is how they view their mistakes.

◆

The best officials turn major problems into small ones, and small problems go unnoticed.

Section 5

Humor

FOUR OF A KIND — 1975, Sabetha, Kansas, 3 sons and their dad officiated a high school game. Left to right: John, referee, Phil, line-judge, Dave, umpire and Dad, headlinesman. This was the first game my father never yelled at the officials, while 3 wives and a mom stood and applauded when we were introduced.

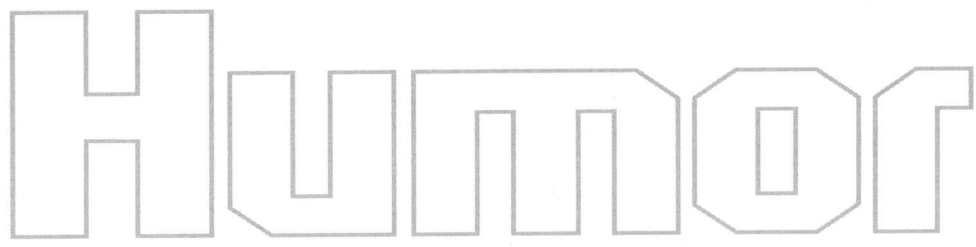

Humor

This is simply the "fun part" of the book. You don't need any background in sports or sports officiating to enjoy some of these quotations. My fear should be that you will either memorize a few and take them to a game, or try one out on an official in person! It takes a sense of humor to be a successful official, and all of us have learned to laugh at ourselves or each other, or we could not have had a long career in sports officiating.

> A football game could have a flag thrown almost every play. Just like the mailman, if he tried to settle down every barking dog, the mail would not get delivered.

> ◆

> If you are going to throw your weight around, be ready to have it thrown around by somebody else, probably bigger and closer to "right" than you.

> ◆

> It is okay to accept an official's mistake and move on. It is a big issue if this official is proud of his stupidity.

> ◆

> An inadvertent whistle should be cremated and not embalmed.

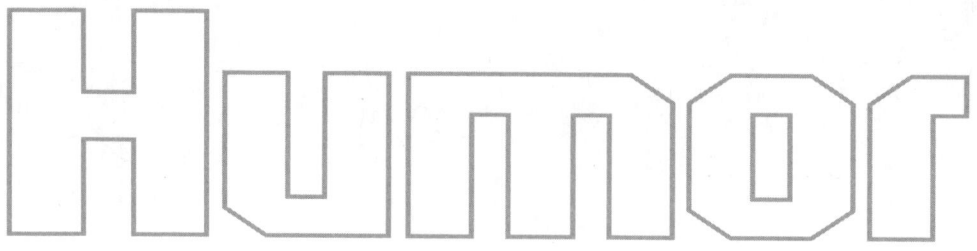

Humor

Be aware of timid officials as they are scared before the game, cowards during the heat of the battle and very courageous in the locker room.

♦

The speed you pick up when you are over-the-hill can not only negatively affect you, but can also cause your crew to ride the slippery slope to the bottom.

♦

If you are interested in bringing attention to yourself, it is hard to beat a good big mistake.

♦

A poorly played football game, in which advantage is unfairly gained, will expand according to the official's willingness to put up with it.

♦

The crisis in the game last Saturday can be a humorous highlight the following week.

Humor

There are two kinds of officials in college football: Those that call the shots, and those that dodge bullets. The ones with the longest careers know when to fire and also when to duck.

◆

Some difficult games to officiate are like a plane flying through a storm. Once you are aboard there is nothing you can do except tighten your belt and hold on.

◆

Some officials choose to take problems on the football field by the horns or by the tail, and some are just along for the ride. But heads usually win and tails always lose.

◆

A good football player is no more a good football official than a drunk is automatically a good bartender.

Humor

The official who can really "sell" a tough call is the same guy who can convince his wife that a fur coat will make her look fat.

◆

If you are in the highlight film at the pre-season meeting, (problem plays from the previous season) it is like being a fire hydrant at a dog convention.

◆

A new crew member who does not improve after the first year is like a baby tiger. Everyone thinks he is cute the first season but he begins to eat your crew the second season.

◆

Some officials are so removed from the real world that when told they are lackadaisical, they simply shrug their shoulders and believe the supervisor is talking about a shortage of flowers.

◆

When officials are considering retirement, consider the tire as the amount of tread left which is more important than mileage.

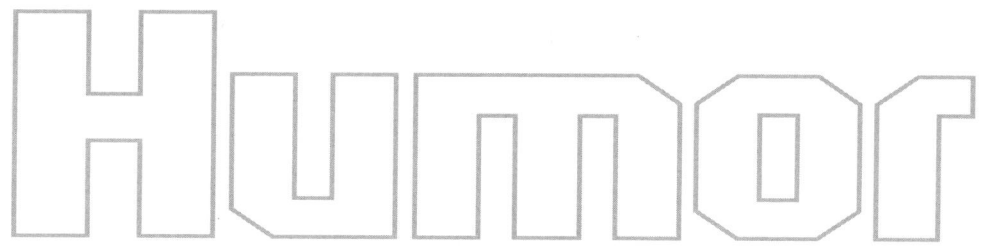

Humor

If your motto as a crew chief is simply "I am going to stay on your ass until your morale improves," it is going to be a long season for everyone.

◆

One in seven Americans has A.D.D. If your crew seems okay, you are it.

◆

Don't approach a goat from the front, a horse from the back or a mad coach any closer than five feet longer than his head set line.

◆

The chief cause of stress in a football game is the reality that you have simply screwed up.

◆

If you are changing your philosophy of "what is a foul" more than you are changing your shirt, keep changing your shirt, just don't put on a black and white striped one anymore.

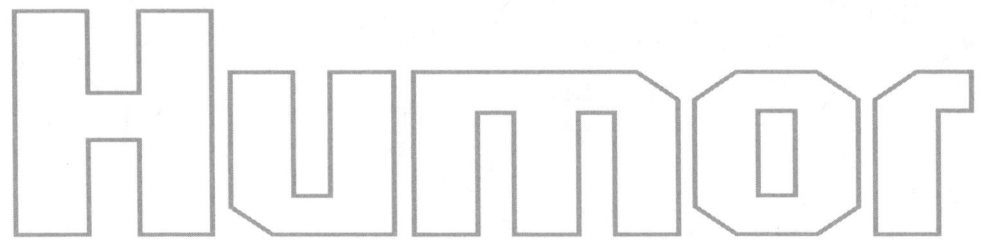

Humor

The crew doesn't care to hear your excuses after the game — It is the guys in the J.V. program who can't wait to talk to you.

♦

If you really think you are important, put on your striped shirt, throw your flag, blow your whistle and try to tell your neighbor's dog what to do.

♦

A survey shows that slender referees have more games than fat ones. The chunky son of the supervisor may be an exception.

♦

A few loose ends during a pregame can give seven men enough rope to hang themselves during a football game.

♦

Some referees take pride in their ability to "B.S." a coach, but remember that officials do not live by words alone and often with too much seasoning in a season they must eat their words.

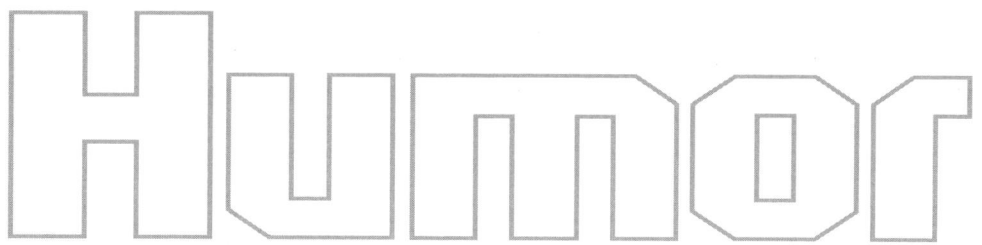

Humor

If you can't accept being criticized as an official, simply quit officiating, become a fan and be as critical as you wish. ✓

———◆———

Three penalties in a row against the non-conference opponent, of a split crew (officials from both conferences) and then having the head linesman tell you that the head coach wants to talk to the referee, is like: The javelin competitor who won the toss and asked to receive.

———◆———

Some officials "on their way up" aren't against you, they are merely for themselves.

———◆———

When everyone in the crowd is "booing" at you, remember half of them are below average. ✓

———◆———

If you have an inadvertent whistle in front of 80,000 fans, if you could, you would simply like to drop dead. Then you would be the happiest official alive.

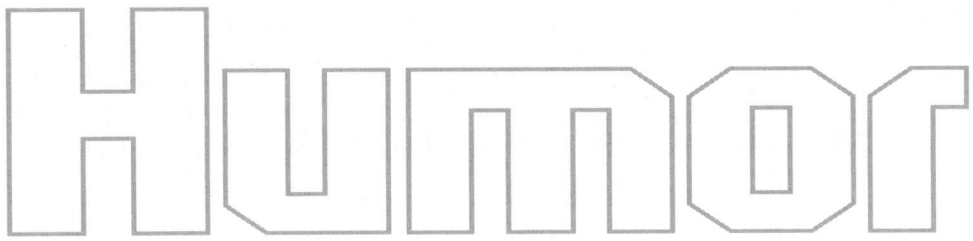

There are three kinds of headlinesmen. Those who count, and those who can't. ✓

———◆———

Rookie officials are predictable, as you never know what inconsistency they're going to do on their next opportunity.

———◆———

Ugly looks bad, but wrong is harder to explain or correct.

———◆———

One of the standing jokes in some conferences is that new officials always spend the first game wondering how they got there and the rest of the season wondering how the experienced officials got there.

———◆———

The difference between picking your nose and "nit-picky" calls: A handkerchief works and a flag doesn't.

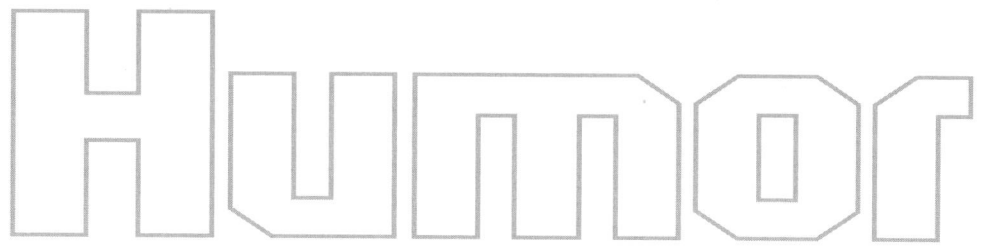

Humor

A referee with the same crew for five weeks, with the same two-hour pregame, probably feels like Liz Taylor's fourth husband — He knows what he is suppose to do, but is at a loss as to how to make it different.

◆

A new pregame without involving the crew is like pissing down your leg. You may think it is hot, but not to anyone else.

◆

A good pregame is a lot like chastity. It is widely praised, but practiced too little.

◆

In the pregame, do what works. If blaming, whining and complaining work, continue to blame, whine and complain. For me, it never worked so I never used them.

◆

When you find out that it takes you a little longer to rest than to get tired, you are ready for the Lazy Boy and TV clicker.

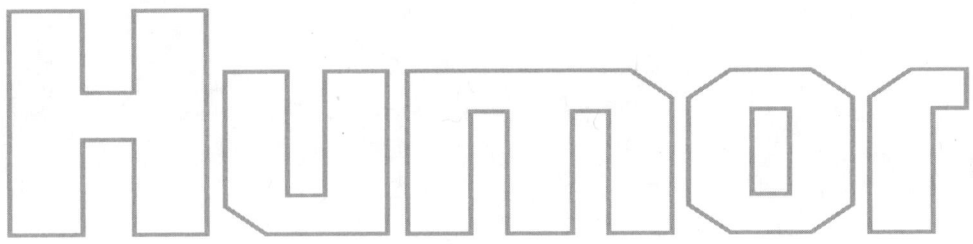

Humor

The short memory of a poorly officiated game is the conscience of an official who will never improve.

———◆———

Some officials have the mentality of cement: Thoroughly mixed up and permanently set beyond change.

———◆———

The hardest job in officiating is trying to look good when you are not.

———◆———

When the "wing" official reports a penalty to the head coach, sometimes he is the bug and sometimes he is the windshield.

———◆———

If you are involved in a "long game," and things aren't going well, it won't do you any good to check your "bowl watch" for the time or think about something after the game. You are no better than your last game — Get focused.

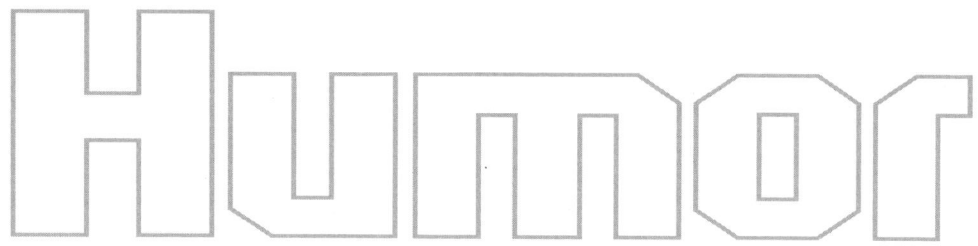

If your crew has a few sacred cow mechanics, they should all probably consider going into the all beef hot dog business.

♦

Your officiating career is that fleeting moment between green and over-ripe.

♦

If you are all wrapped up in yourself, your uniform is too big and the package is very small.

♦

Don't be in a hurry to make decisions or blow your whistle, as skating over thin ice quickly can get you in hot water.

♦

Don't hurl defiance unless your aim is good and your career is over.

♦

Officials are just like some wines that improve with age. The grapes must be good in the first place and the official must have potential.

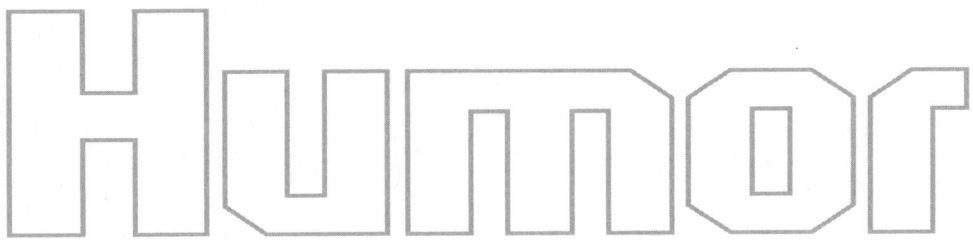

When tensions are high, don't boil...Keep cool, but also don't freeze.

◆

For my friends who have been on my crews from Texas...If I owned hell and Texas, I'd rent out Texas and live in hell. Attributed to: P.J. Sheridan

◆

The halo for last week's game is only about six inches higher than next week's potential noose.

◆

Common sense and sense of humor are important in officiating... A sense of humor is simply good timing for common sense.

◆

A good solution to a difficult situation is better than the perfect one discovered in the post-game discussion.

◆

Some overweight talkative officials do not live by words alone, even though they must eat them most of the time.

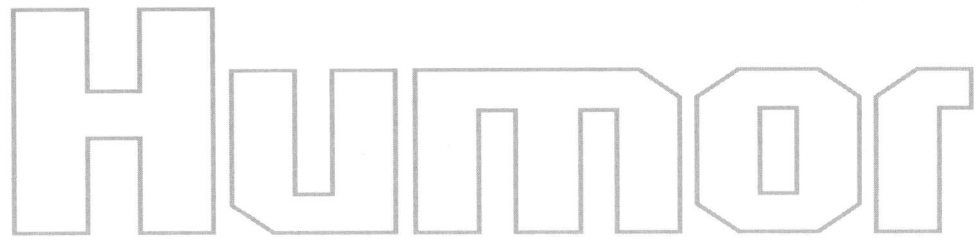

Humor

An old wood is best to burn, old horses to ride, old books to read, old wine to drink, old umpires for good judgment, old friends are trusty to use — Everything else "old" should retire. ✓

◆

As bad as you are humiliated on national TV, just remember that it is only someone else's momentary entertainment.

◆

Throwing your flag after seeing what looked like a foul because of the way the play ended, is like a man who goes into a dark cellar at midnight without a light, looking for a black cat that was never there.

◆

Fourth and goal at the one…Last play of the game…Score tied: A bunch of wet spaghetti or backbone?

◆

Every official will probably be a poor official for about one minute during a football game. The key is not to exceed your limit.

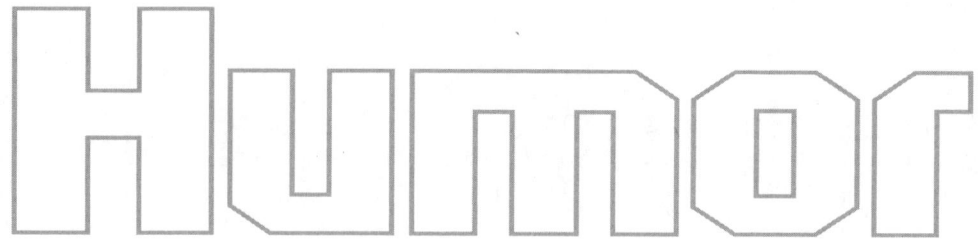

See the play…Make the call…Don't be caught up with paralysis through over-analysis.

———◆———

In some games you simply must accept the bitter with the sour.

———◆———

If your mind-set before the game is that "It is going to be a bad game" — You have a great chance of being a prophet. ✓

———◆———

If you believe you have worked a great game, and the only admiration you are getting is your dog wagging his tail…Check the game tape.

———◆———

When an official has been totally screened out, yet must make the call (you can tell this because his eyes look like saucers), somebody needs to throw a rope and pull him out — Just not both ends.

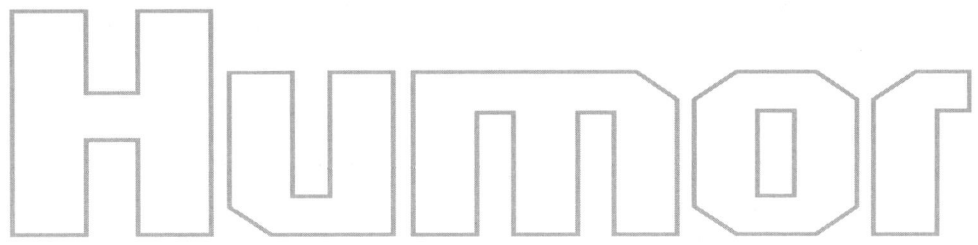

Humor

The potential of an inadvertent whistle is but a short breath of air that would fill a balloon. But that difference is one of a padded seat in the locker room at a bowl game and a recliner in front of the TV on New Year's Day.

———◆———

Bring your crew up to a professional level… Surrounding yourself with dwarfs does not make you a giant.

———◆———

Be careful of a referee nicknamed Jigsaw, as every time a flag is thrown he goes to pieces.

———◆———

If the crew conference has seven shovels digging a hole, first stop digging. Then look for what is best by rule. If necessary decide what is fair, or which team was disadvantaged.

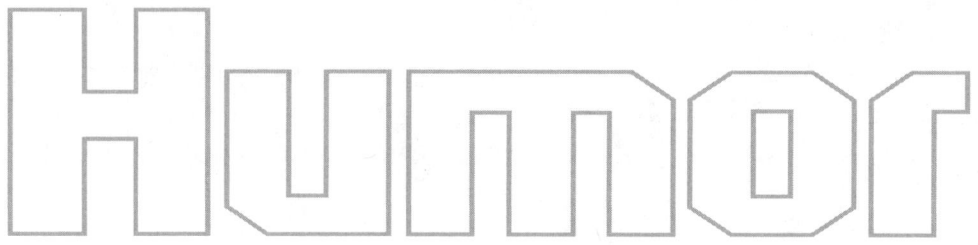

Humor

When you are trying to get the press to understand a particular call or situation in a game, it is very much like having a picnic with a tiger… You might enjoy the meal, but the tiger always eats last.

◆

The more hot dogs on the field, the more banana peels. Keep the dogs wrapped and watch where you step. (This one requires quite a bit of imagination; I apologize to the serious official.)

◆

Tunnel-vision officiating is like looking at the sky through a straw.

◆

Finding out information after the game that could have corrected a mistake, is like going in after the war has been lost and bayoneting the wounded.

◆

There are three kinds of happenings in a crew on any one play. Some know, some watch and some wonder. The referee must sort through all three and make the right decision.

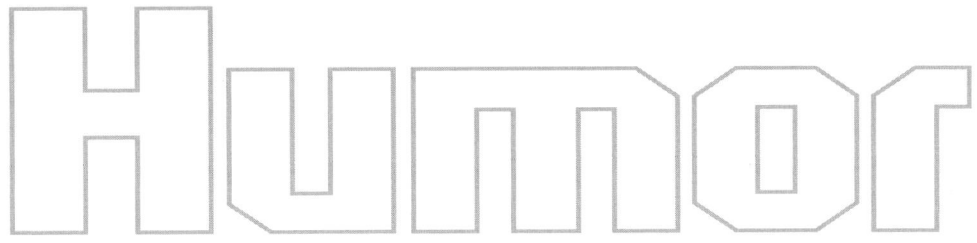

During a tough game, after everyone has had a chance to conform to the rules, remember: You never tame a tiger by stroking it.

―◆―

Once a game gets out of control, and breakdowns have occurred between the teams, crew and coaches, it is like trying to put toothpaste back in the tube — Control the flow of the game.

―◆―

Don't enter Folsom Field (Colorado) unless you can cross the field in 9.9 seconds. Ralphie, the Colorado buffalo, can do it in 10 seconds. Or, don't step on the field to officiate unless you have prepared to do your best. Stay ahead of the teams and the coaches.

―◆―

If you really want to advise me, do it on Saturday afternoon between 1:00 and 4:00. And you've got 25 seconds to do it, between plays. Not on Monday. I know the right thing to do on Monday. Alex Agase, football coach

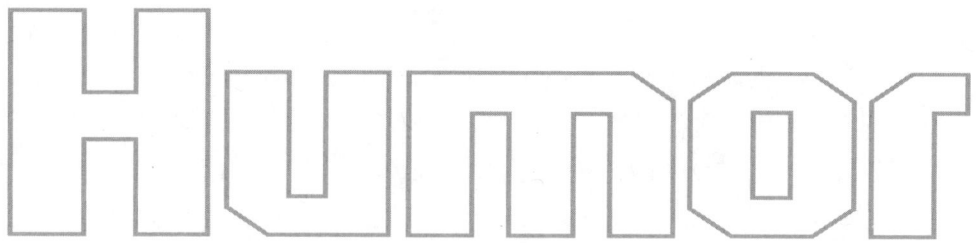

Humor

When the candles cost more than the cake, don't wait for a blow out to retire.

◆

The best officials don't let their wheels show.

◆

The anatomy of how to officiate a good football game can be dissected, just as a frog can be, but everything dies in the process. (Every good football game has a flow and feeling of momentum that cannot be explained by dissection.)

◆

Many young officials consider themselves as experienced, excellent officials and are content. That's the reason there are so few experienced, excellent officials.

◆

Some sports writers: A jumbo hot dog filled with ink.

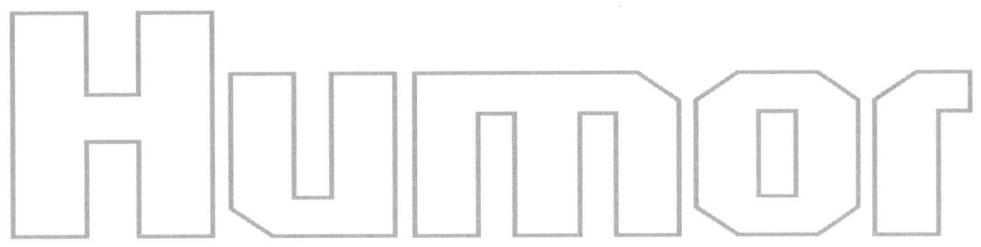

Humor

Two ways to rise to the top of officiating: 1). You can work and earn it. 2). Crap floats to the top. (#2 will only work in the toilet bowl.)

———◆———

You can generally tell when you are officiating a good football game because it is a lot like sonar. When you hear noise from both sidelines, you know you are on course and doing a good job. ✓

———◆———

The real challenge of a football game is to make a solid foundation from the bricks thrown by players, coaches and the fans. Avoid the distractions and build from what is given you.

———◆———

A tough football game to officiate is war minus the shooting.

———◆———

Be aware of the officials who have an excuse for everything. They prefer to shoot the arrow and then draw the bull's eye where it lands.

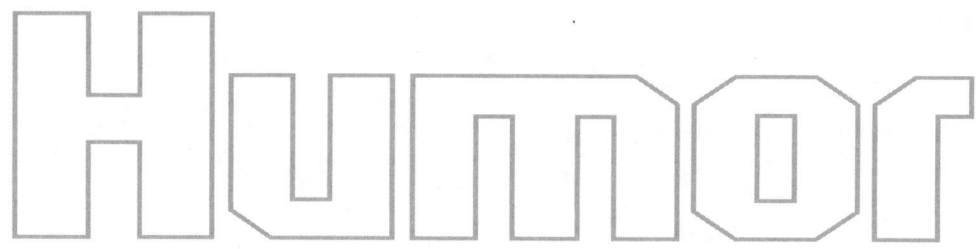

Humor

If you tell someone that you just "worked the perfect game," and you are not ashamed, you have not been honest twice.

◆

Some officials are designed to screw up the simplest plays in football. If they were given a hot dog, they would eat the catsup bottle.

◆

Solution to an inadvertent whistle: don't make the same mistake once.

◆

The best officials make mistakes. The poor officials make more, and the most miserable simply are the habitual indecisive type.

◆

Officials who back into the limelight, eventually shine on the back side.

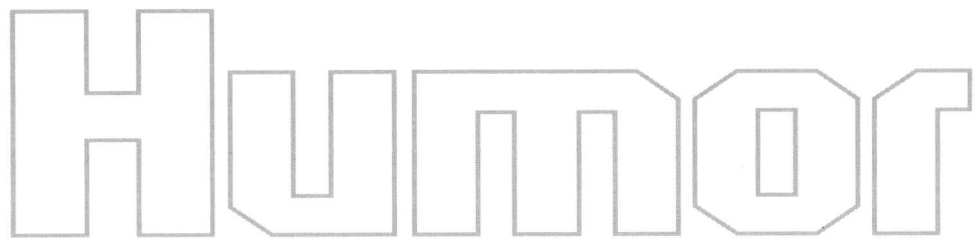

Humor

The quickest way to get in trouble in a football game is to redouble your effort when you have forgotten your direction.

◆

Some officials simply mature late and some simply rot early. Try to mature early and improve.

◆

If you are involved in a "pool reporter" post-game activity after a tough game, never underestimate the power of a stupid journalist in a large group.

◆

Some games the referee needs to put the game on "cruise control." Some games require brakes, sometimes a horn, sometimes a ticket. Don't take the game away from the players, just avoid losing control and "accidents."

◆

The official on the crew who boasts that he has worked a game in which he has never made a mistake, has a referee who did.

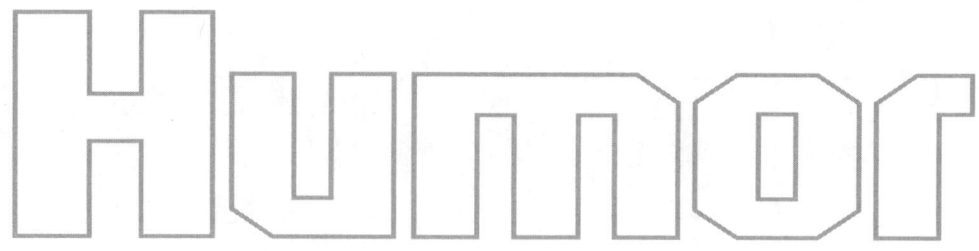

Humor

If every member of the crew is "in it for themselves," the castrated crew will have no "off spring" (spring games) and will probably be "off the field" the next fall.

◆

If within your crew you are the gold filling in a mouth of decay, you need to be extracted and the crew needs false teeth.

◆

A self-centered official never takes an eye off of himself.

◆

Animal house officiating: Trying to keep order in the zoo, led by a crew of zebras and one ass.

◆

My father told me not to bet my bladder against the brewery, or to get into an argument with a coach who knows the rules.

◆

To keep a good flow to a football game, good officials read between the lines of the rule book.

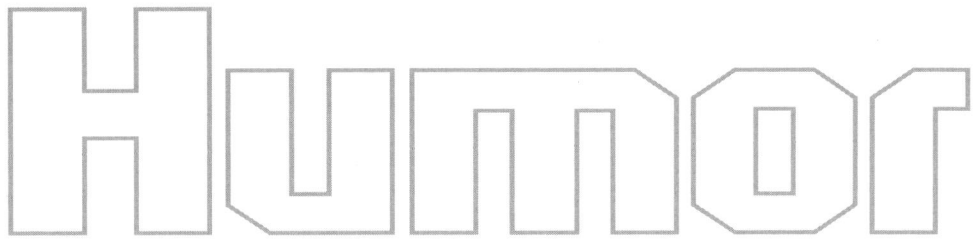

Humor

If weather distracts you as a football official, stick to basketball.

♦

Officials seeking revenge from other officials or coaches find an empty fullness that is similar to eating Astro-Turf.

♦

An incorrect call is generally more of a critical mistake than not making the call, but too many of either of these calls will require a calling different than officiating.

♦

You can always tell a rule book official, you just can't tell him much.

♦

A "book official" who is faultless to a fault, can take the "flow of the game" away from both teams.

♦

You can sharpen your game by reading the rule book, but the real test is chopping wood after the kick off.

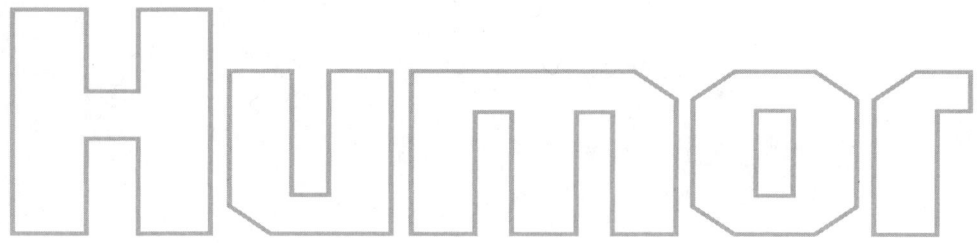

Ignorance of the rules is not an excuse, but it is a statement.

―◆―

Beware of the coach who gives you the "V" sign during a heated contest. As, when you turn around, he may forget about one finger.

―◆―

It doesn't help to "turn the other cheek" when you have said the wrong thing to the coach if your tongue is still in the way.

―◆―

Never trust a coach with short legs as his brain is too close to his butt.

―◆―

Is the coach really swearing at you if he simply says "Be fruitful and multiply?"

―◆―

Mediocrity is the hand-rail for those poor officials whose goal is simply to "stay on their feet."

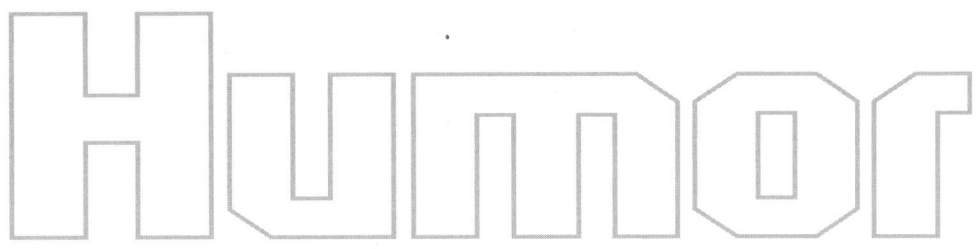

Humor

Keep in mind when visiting with a very upset coach still wearing his headphones; he is getting prejudiced information that you can't hear, and also being supported or hated by probably more fans than live in your hometown.

◆

I like paranoid coaches because they actually feel like officials are paying attention to them.

◆

A book official will lie to a coach to explain a rule interpretation that he has been waiting a year to create.

◆

I have seen a few umpires and head coaches that simply look like they have just swallowed an entire human being.

◆

Cab drivers, like "book officials," prove that practice does not make perfect.

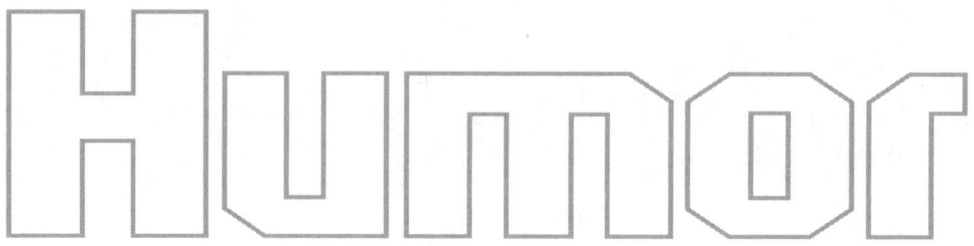

Humor

Some officials are simply born to suck the poison out of every part of the rule book, instead of using it as medicine to cure a sick game.

◆

Make sure if you are "kicked upstairs" to the NFL, that it is not a one-story building.

◆

If there is not a fair solution to a complicated problem on the field, simply admire the problem and move on.

◆

The special quality of great official is they do their best when they simply dislike what is going on.

◆

Be careful of the official who tells you he is not always right, but he is never wrong. (This is a little like the baseball umpire saying "It isn't a strike until I call it.")

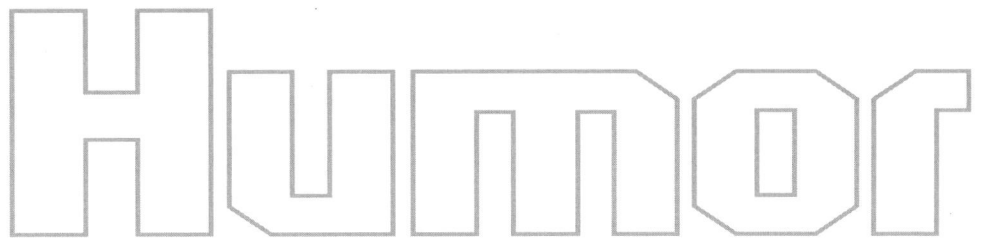

Humor

The aspirin official: This guy tries to solve every problem (illness) with the same solution (medicine) without understanding the game.

———◆———

The best way to describe an official who unfairly has worked his way through the ranks of officiating is to simply call him an authentic phony.

———◆———

When an official has climbed the ladder of success, it is unpleasant to say, but sometimes his fellow officials may be shaking the ladder.

———◆———

Rationalizing plays, looking the other way, and following the path of least resistance is what makes rivers crooked and officials weak.

———◆———

Some officials would rather be a big fish in a small pond, and some would rather be the head of nothing than the tail of something. (Go back to your day job, or find another crew if you are caught here.)

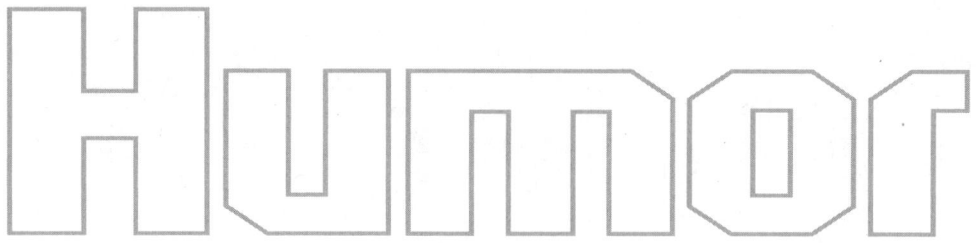

Humor

A soft head and a hard heart simply mean a hard ending to a soft career.

◆

If your elevator of success flows down or stops during the season, take the stairs.

◆

If after five years of officiating you are not working varsity games, think about modifying your dreams or magnifying your skills.

◆

If you have officiated for five years and made no enemies, you are a failure.

◆

You can never talk yourself out of problems that you have behaved yourself into.

◆

Having an inadvertent whistle in a game isn't the worst thing that can happen, as long as it does not happen to you.

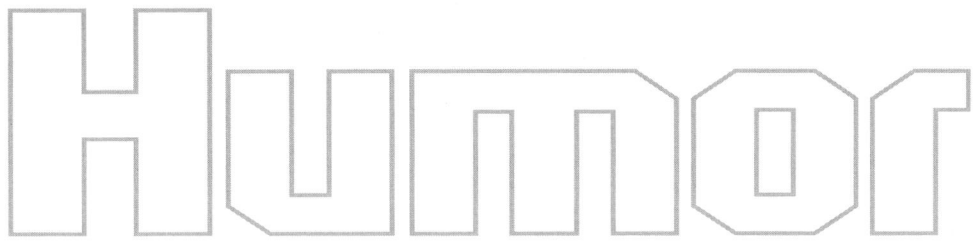

If you are simply a black and white official, trade in your color TV and watch Bowl Games from your Lazy Boy.

❖

Martyrdom is the only way in which an official can become famous without ability.

❖

The ability to officiate without ambition is like a car without a motor.

❖

Some coaches and officials are sure of their facts even though they never happened.

❖

The center of attention at a football game should be the players during the game, the band at half time, maybe the cheerleaders, and never the coach or officials.

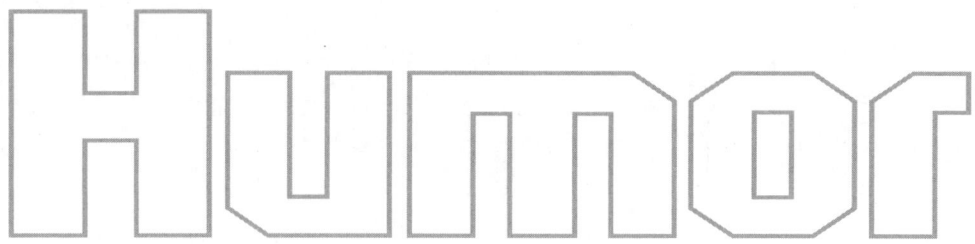

Humor

Some officials' "movement" on the field is so bad, they might have better luck eating alphabet soup and spelling out m.o.v.e.m.e.n.t. on the other end.

◆

Non-conference games are not a dress rehearsal.

◆

What a lot of rookie officials and coaches don't know about football would make a good rule book.

◆

Some officials are so consistent, their indecision is final.

◆

Reading the rule book doesn't make you a good official any more than going to the garage makes you a car.

◆

Some officials believe they are so good, modesty is their best quality.

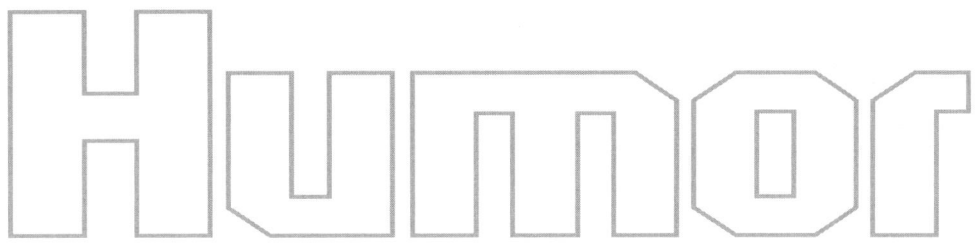

Humor

Jealousy: All of the fun you think those who wanted to take your place had while reviewing your latest mistake on replay.

Keep in mind that your most embarrassing mistake of the season, which included serious emotional chaos, will later be remembered and toasted over a cold beer.

A macho official does not prove mucho.

Some officials have problems with coaches because their neuroses simply don't match.

Football rules are no more written for football officials than ghost stories are written for ghosts.

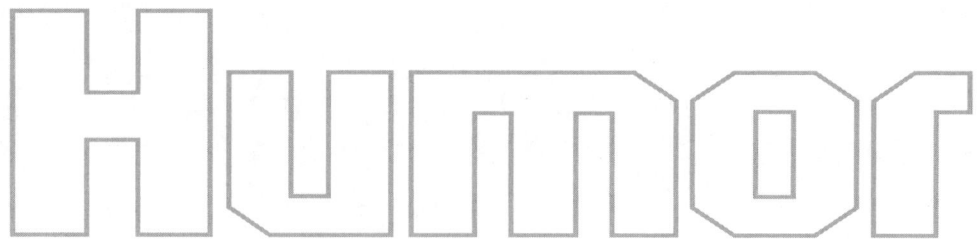

Humor

"Coach, I know you believe you understood what you think I said, but I'm not sure you realize that what you heard is not what I meant to say." If the coach remains confused, feel lucky and walk away.

◆

Sometimes the very best thing you can say about a negative crew member is that at least he stabbed you in the front.

◆

We are having such a bad game without you as our referee, it is almost like having you here.

◆

Some officials look like they have been poured into their uniform and forgot to say "when."

◆

Sometimes officials don't know the meaning of the word courage but when you get to know them you find they don't know the meaning of most words.

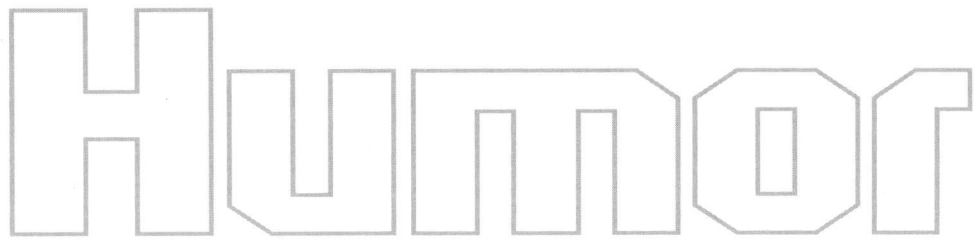

Humor

Some games simply get a lot worse before they get a lot worse.

---◆---

Officials whose hat size increases throughout the football season, usually have shoes which are easy to fill.

---◆---

Some frustrations in a football game are like trying to find your glasses, without your glasses.

---◆---

Next time you "wipe it off" because you didn't see the play, you are moving slowly from the dog house to the out house.

---◆---

Officials can be measured in layers when the crap is piled on during the game. Layer by layer, the very best officials and crews turn it into fertilizer for the remainder of the game.

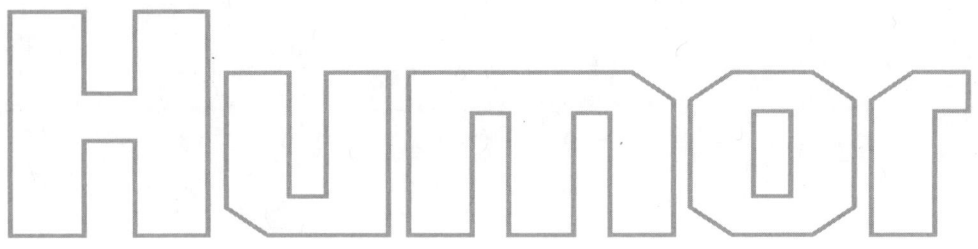

Humor

Get to know the quality of the character of the coaches you are working with during a game as it is impossible to defeat an ignorant coach in an argument.

◆

If you have done a poor job in a game and you are being complimented by a "wannabe" in the league, keep in mind that deep down they are hoping to take your place.

◆

The only sound that travels faster than sound is an inadvertent whistle.

◆

Inexperienced officials remember everything, whether it happened or not. Retired officials simply remember the latter.

◆

Trying to communicate with an irate coach is as easy as threading a sewing machine needle when it is operating at full speed.

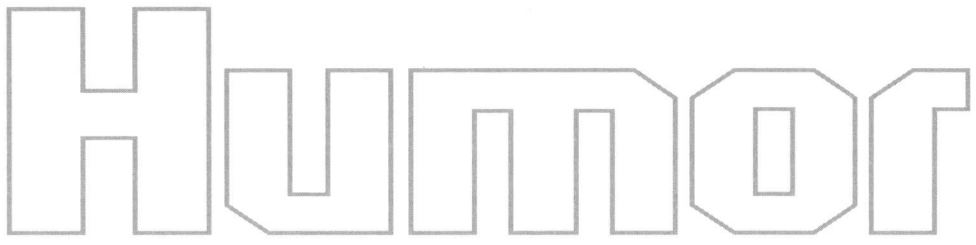

Humor

Sometimes a coach's gestures and "silence" is fun to watch and fun to listen too.

―◆―

At least half of the lies coaches tell about officials are not true.

―◆―

See leather before you blow the whistle, or you may next season feel leather from your Lazy Boy while watching the game on TV.

―◆―

The most difficult coaches that I have ever met do not have a single redeeming defect. OK, maybe one or two.

―◆―

Besides being penalized 15 yards for calling me a "sonofabitch," the coach has never met my mother.

―◆―

There are more comic strip characters in the coaching area along the sidelines of a football game than in the newspaper.

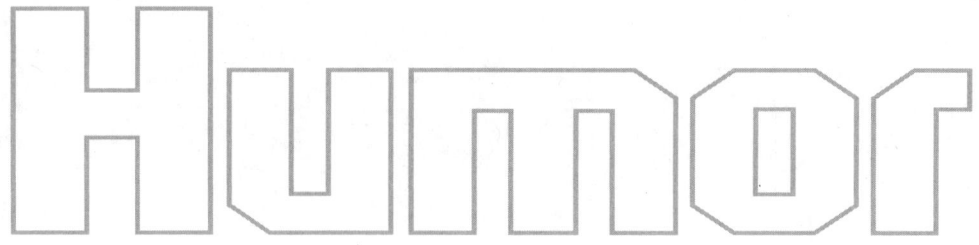

Humor

The strictest interpretation of the rule is not always the best interpretation for a football game.

◆

It is what you learn after you know the rule book that counts.

◆

The best officials tend to think in grooves and rhythm and want a flow to the game rather than what happens on each play.

◆

When an official is "too big" to study the rule book, he has out-grown his ability to improve.

◆

It does no good to know the rules if you can't "pull the trigger" on the field.

◆

100% on the rules test does not ensure wisdom on the field.

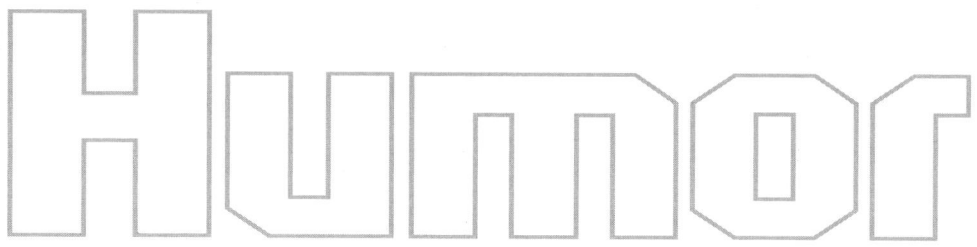

Humor

Lots of officials can get the right answer when sitting at a desk, even with the rule book in view. It is the on-field decisions and being wise on time that makes things a little more difficult.

---◆---

If you want to propose to a coach, use these three words, "I love you." If you have made a mistake use these three words to gain respect, "I was wrong."

---◆---

In some officiating circles, (sorry Texas) politeness is the most Southern acceptable form of hypocrisy.

---◆---

One of the heaviest burdens an official can carry when confronted by a coach, is to have a chip on his shoulder.

---◆---

No matter how thin you slice a mistake, it is still baloney.

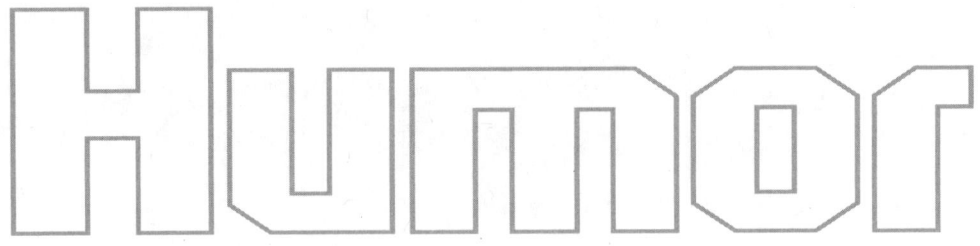

Humor

Out of the mouths of babes comes — Cereal; and from officials who swear at players or coaches — A shortened career.

―◆―

When the coach says, "I agree with you, great call," my first thought is that I must have missed the call.

―◆―

Is an "abnormal official" anyone who behaves differently than you?

―◆―

The most important thing in officiating is decisiveness. If you can fake it, you've got it made.

―◆―

Blowing the whistle to get players' attention works sometimes, but always works when the ball is still "alive."

―◆―

Bad conditions don't bother good officials. Some officials are like sun dials and simply don't function during a rain.

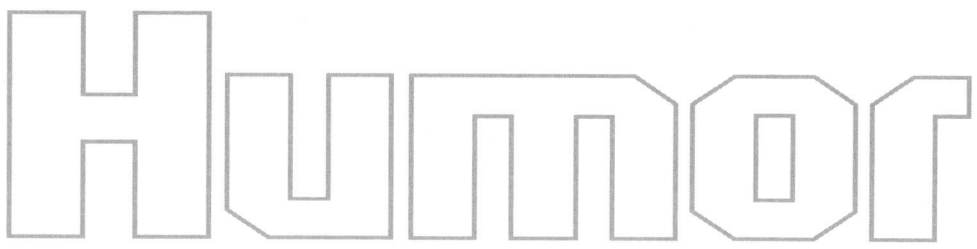

Humor

Never try to tell a coach everything you know about a football ruling for two reasons: 1) His attention span may be short. 2) You may end up telling him more than you know.

◆

Don't be angry with a coach who is smarter than you — It is not his fault.

◆

A "white hat" and an "R" on the back of a shirt makes some grow and some sweat.

◆

The only thing some officials can do better than anyone else is to read their own handwriting.

◆

The "metallic age" of officiating: Gold in your teeth, silver in your hair, and lead in your pants.

◆

When you are in an argument with a coach and one of you is acting like a fool, be careful because the media may not be able to tell the difference.

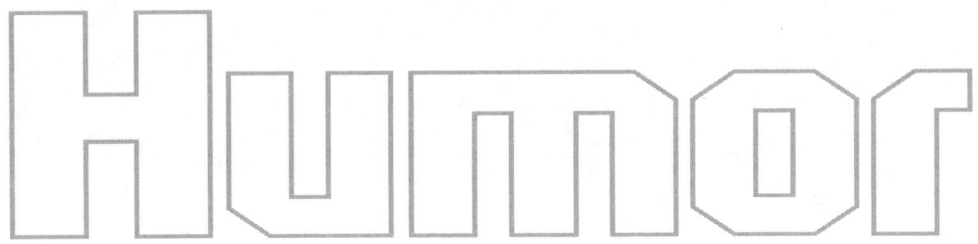

Humor

Every mistake made on the field has an "I" and every excuse has a "U."

―◆―

Some crews display a lot of talent when it comes to acting like a bunch of lost zebras.

―◆―

If you are a poor official, you don't have to worry about making a comeback.

―◆―

After a big-time mistake in the game, humble pie has a bitter taste, but it can also provide nourishment.

―◆―

Never disagree with a doctor or instant replay official, as they both have "inside" information.

―◆―

Beware of the crew gossiper, as he can burn a scandal at both ends.

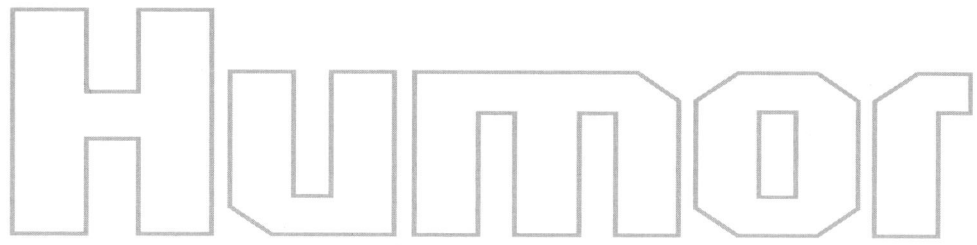

Humor

A crew with a little humor when gathering to make a difficult decision can be a tranquilizer with no negative side effects.

The best referees can step on crew members' toes without messing up their shine.

Never bury a mad dog by sticking his tail out of the ground, or take a cheap shot at a coach when you move from him to the center of the field.

When an official tells you that he has "learned from his mistakes" be careful that he is not actually telling you that he is learning to make more.

Some officials are so narrow minded that their peripheral vision is vertical.

Beware of the J.V. official who falls at your feet as he may be reaching to pull the rug out from under you.

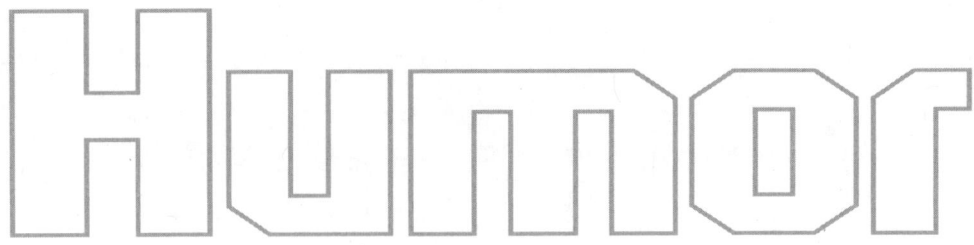

Humor

Flattery from an official wanting to take your place is the way a wolf looks at a dog.

◆

If you can't run with the dogs, stay off the porch or go upstairs and do replay.

◆

Some officials uniforms have the distinguishing look of "failure."

◆

It is difficult to describe some officials as "has beens," when a better description is "never will be."

◆

His "statisticals" were not large enough to handle the pressure of the game.

◆

When the "stuff" hits the fan, you define the moment, or the moment will "splatter" all over you!

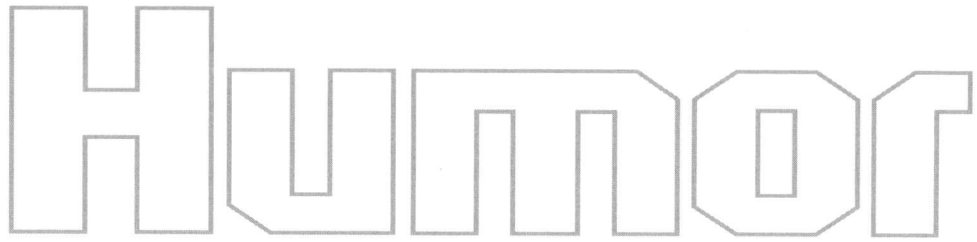

Humor

If a crew member tries to "pull the rug out from under you" in front of a coach, try dancing around it on the Astro-Turf and then "clean house" later.

◆

The feeling of having an inadvertent whistle is about the same as having a heart attack while playing charades!

Section 6

Leadership

International presentation on block scheduling, Sydney, Australia. (Dr. Laurie has made presentations in 37 states and 4 foreign countries on the topic of block scheduling.)

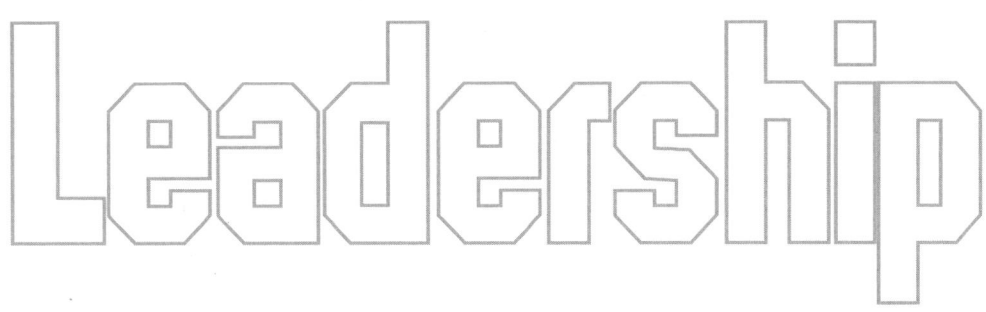

Leadership

You will find quotations about leadership also in the Referee chapter of this book, as there is an obvious overlap. Individual leadership is very important for each member of an officiating crew or a member of an organization. This section is directed towards "leadership" in general, and is specifically addressed in the referee chapter.

When there is confusion on the field, action is the best remedy to regain control.

◆

Difficulties have a tendency to vanish when officials take charge of the game and face them boldly.

◆

Consensus building is not the part of leadership that a referee uses when a decision needs to be made on the field. No votes, no approach on which everyone agrees — Get the facts and make the call.

◆

The best solution to some problems on the field that can't be solved, is to simply manage them.

Leadership

Rivalry between crews is much healthier than envy between crews. Just as cooperation is a more productive quality than competition between crews.

◆

Some officials appear so cocky — They look as if they could strut sitting down.

◆

When problems occur in a crew in which the leader does not take charge, six crew members become like beads on a string and slip off one at a time.

◆

Be humble and remember your purpose as an official. Some officials become so pompous and self-made, they worship their creator.

◆

Sometimes during a game, it is difficult to see a clear decision and you must simply take the least blurred.

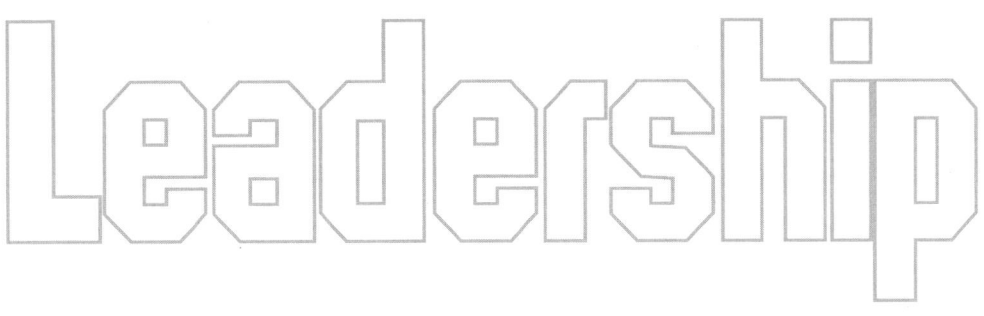

Some officials have a tendency to obscure the forest of the good flow of the game with "trees" of problems.

◆

During a crew conversation over a tough call, sometimes the best information you have is a collective hunch.

◆

Expect a few problems in the game and then eat them for breakfast.

◆

Consistently poor officiating is better than inconsistent officiating. But when an official's indecision is his final decision, the game is in real trouble.

◆

Sometimes a kick-in-the-butt is a step forward (if hard enough) for some officials in some situations.

◆

Officiating a great game is a great teacher. Working through adversity is even a greater teacher.

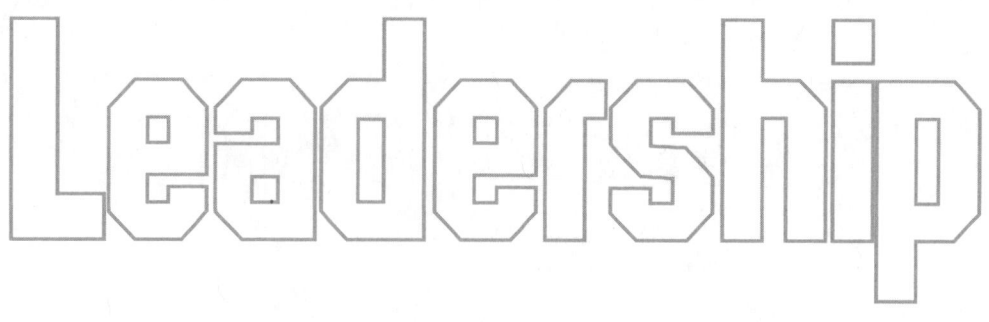

Leadership

Changing talent to ability is the key to a referee successfully making a good crew and great crew.

◆

In a tough situation, thought and theory are important, but you reach a point where taking action prevails.

◆

When in a conversation with a coach, you can afford to keep your temper when you are right, and you can't afford to lose it when you are wrong.

◆

A leaderless crew provides an equal opportunity for everyone to be incompetent.

◆

The emphasis during a tough crisis on the field must be, "What's wrong and how do we correct it?" Not "who's the blame for this mess"?

◆

The necessity of making a big call in a big game can even make the timid brave.

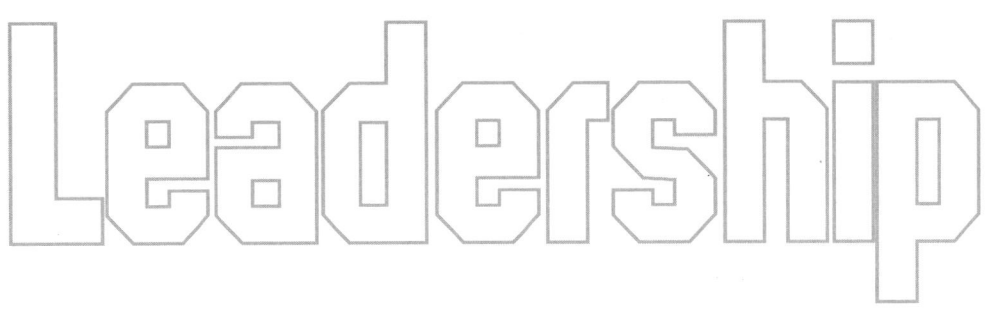

Leadership

When being proactive and preventative in officiating, wear gloves, but when it comes time to take control of the game, be barefisted.

♦

The tough choices are not usually black or white, but shades of terrible gray. Gather good information and un-mix the shades of gray.

♦

The shortest solution to a difficult situation is to simply do it.

♦

Indecision is often worse than wrong action.

♦

When reviewing a complex situation on the field, think about common sense and substance, and don't try to grasp at a possible fleeting shadow because it looks good.

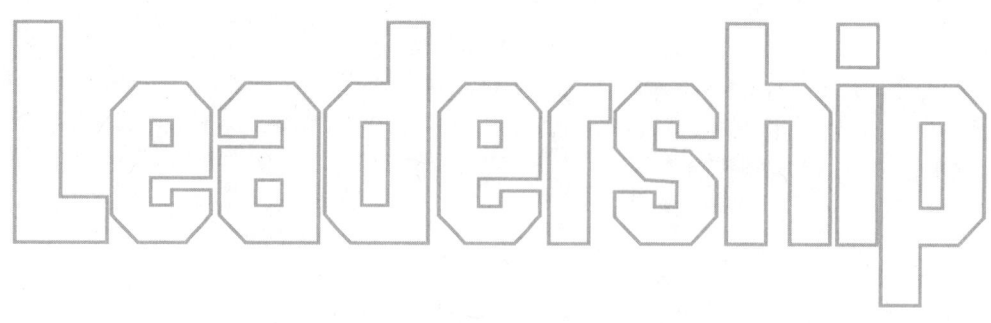

Leadership

There is power in the striped shirt. The influence is the key and it is: character, reputation and communication. It is what is under the shirt that separates officials.

◆

From a leadership perspective for a referee, a mean streak is an important quality to have…Knowing when to use it is the key.

◆

Every referee needs to test his leadership abilities. When his opinion is in the minority, it does test his courage; and when it is with the majority of the crew, it tests his tolerance.

◆

More than one crew chief (referee) in a crew will eventually cause the group to fail for lack of unity.

◆

In that moment of uncertainty, the key is how you handle that slight impulse that directs you one way or the other. Some have this, and some will never learn it.

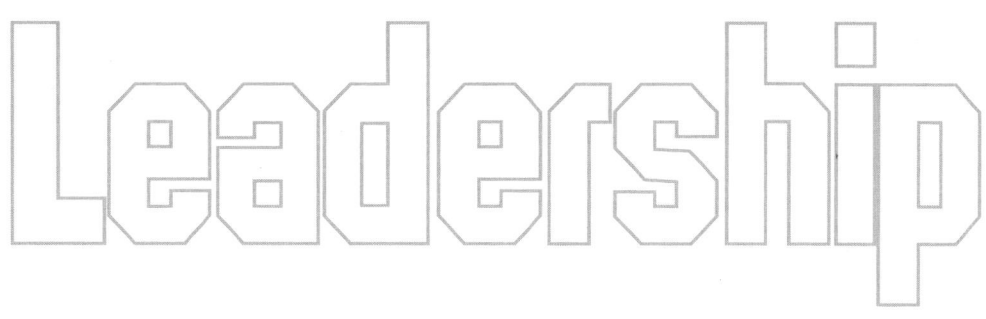

Leadership

Be careful of overusing your authority to your crew or the head coach…The more you use, the less you have.

◆

When working with a poor official, always try to advise and counsel him, and if that does not work, allow adversity to teach him the lesson. The problem, of course, is that he won't get many lessons.

◆

When the game has a few pot holes, crews work in cruise control.

◆

It is possible that crew agreement simply means that everyone got it wrong.

◆

When crisis occurs on the field, stay focused and try to keep drama from entering the scene while the situation is being resolved.

Leadership

A crew conference can be dangerous if agreement is reached on only one discussed option.

———◆———

Tolerance/over-the-edge: The best officials have a feel for this timing and simply know when to pull the trigger and when to pass.

———◆———

Common sense is more than having the crew agree with you (referee). It is sometimes not a majority opinion, but getting the play right.

———◆———

If you let the crew make decisions that the referee is supposed to make, you will be trampled.

———◆———

Leadership is action, not position. An "R" on your back does not make you a leader.

———◆———

Success in a controversial situation belongs to the official, who after other crew members have let go, hangs on and solves the problem.

Leadership

Kansas State University, Dr. Kent Stewart, Chair of the Department of School Administration.

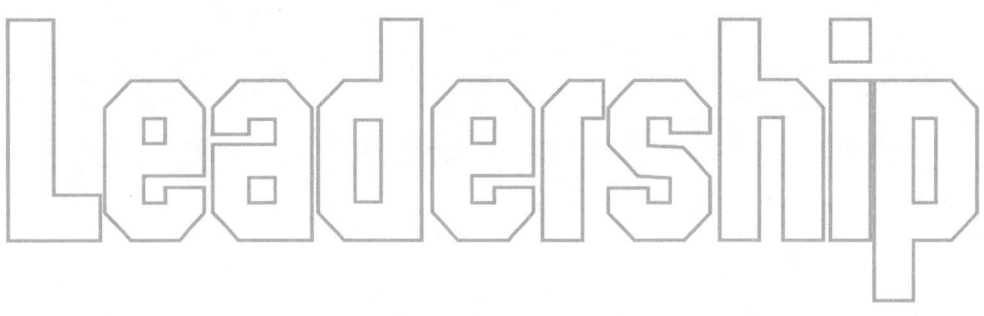

Leadership

A good crew is the arrow, the referee aims and releases the bow, and the score is shared by the crew.

◆

Some referees leave no doubt by allowing their mannerisms to show they have no value in crew team work.

◆

A dull leader breeds a dull crew.

◆

There is no accompaniment for a crew when they are each singing their own praises.

◆

When you are confronted with an impossible situation, still look for possibilities.

◆

The opportunity to get a tough play right will shrink or expand depending on ones character and presence on the field.

Leadership

Officials with courage have a special kind of knowledge. They simply know what to fear out of respect and what not to fear respectfully.

◆

The ability to lead a crew as a referee is an attitude before it is ability.

◆

There is a testing point in almost every game where game officials have a chance to demonstrate appropriate courage.

◆

Officials with charisma have the ability to transfer their enthusiasm to others.

◆

You can dodge responsibility but not the consequence of your responsibility.

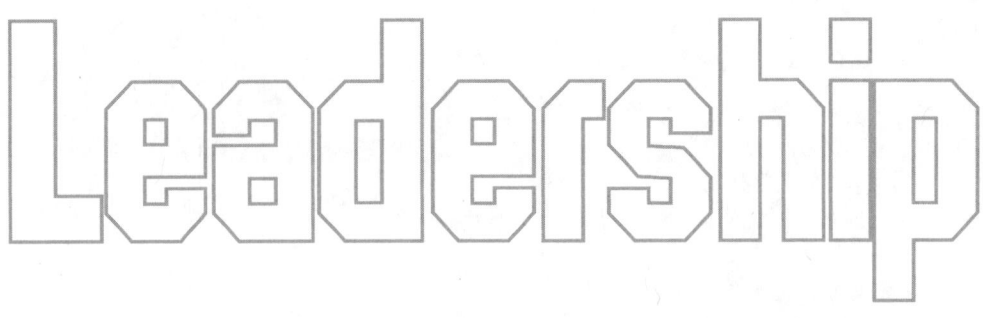

Leadership

"You must be the worst referee in the world," said the dejected umpire after a terrible game. "I doubt it," replied the referee, "That would be too much of a coincidence."

---◆---

Leadership is not the "R" on the referee's back, but his actions with the crew.

---◆---

In a crew conference, don't find blame, but fix the problem.

---◆---

One bad attitude in a crew is infectious. The good news is that a positive attitude is also infectious to a crew.

---◆---

Some crews during a difficult crew conference spend too little time on the problem and too much time determining which official to blame.

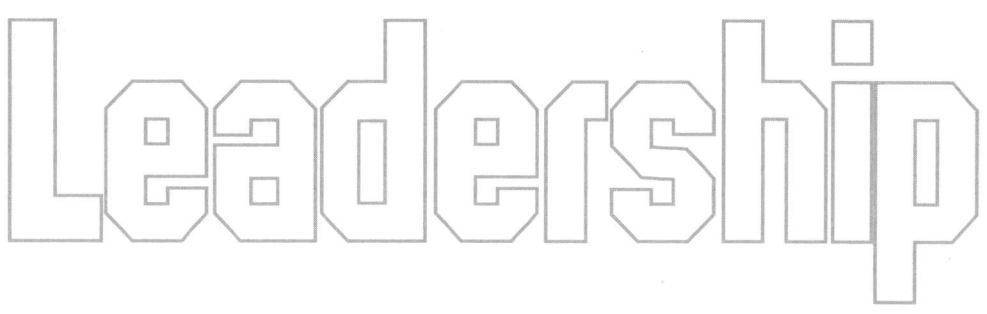

Leadership

Having on-going optimism is a force multiplier for the crew.

---◆---

Sometimes to conquer a very difficult game, you need to make up your mind that you are going to simply endure the situation.

---◆---

During an emotional crew conference, simply gathering important information does not guarantee good judgment.

---◆---

In a heated crew discussion over a controversial issue, don't allow the crew to find fault; find a remedy.

---◆---

A part of controlling a difficult game is to learn to create a positive flow to a series of "little things."

---◆---

Effective officials have two items to get the attention and respect from coaches: 1) Long and short sticks and 2) Long and short carrots.

Leadership

The best reason for taking the "straight and narrow" path in your officiating career, is that very few actually pass you.

———◆———

First accept the situation and then overcome the problem.

———◆———

A reputation of your officiating skills is built the first ten years; your character is established during the next ten.

———◆———

Beware of the official who is always asking you for advice, often he is simply asking for praise.

———◆———

If you are good enough to tell someone, you don't need to.

———◆———

When the game you have worked speaks for itself, don't interrupt it to show your "control" or "presence."

Section 7

Loyalty
(Teamwork)

Last game together on the field — my brother Phil and our father (Dave), Oklahoma @ Nebraska, 1999.

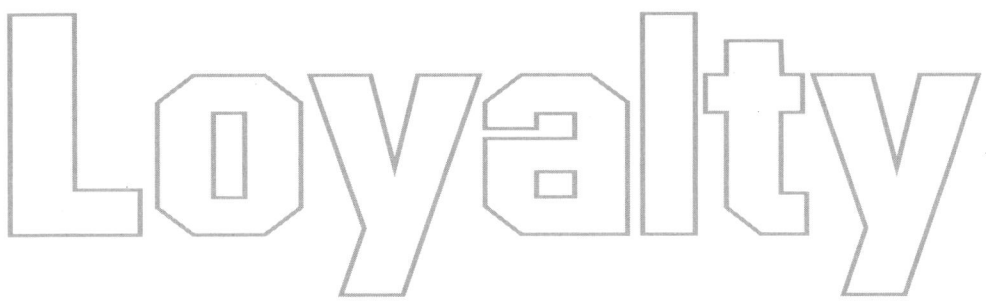

Loyalty and teamwork are the two working parts of an officiating crew as well as any organization organized into "teams." When officiating a game in which there is a lot of individualized and collective pressure on the crew; loyalty and teamwork always come to the surface of successful officiating teams and organizations.

Good officials can uncomplicate difficult situations, and poor officials make simple situations complex.

◆

The more often a crew acts foolish, the greater chance it is not an act.

◆

At some point each official must carry his part of the load. Continuing to "spoon feed" a new official only teaches him the shape of the silver spoon.

◆

A crew with a weak official who refuses to improve is like a bucket with a hole in it; sooner or later the bucket (crew) will run dry.

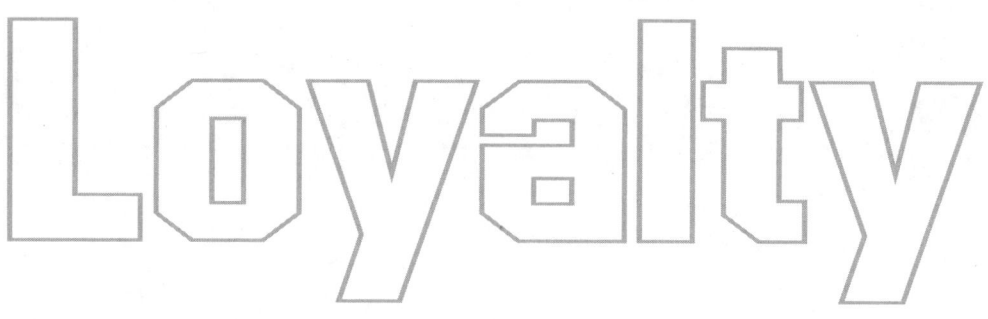

Loyalty

When judging other officials, it is a good idea to remember how much easier it is to be critical than correct.

◆

When you have key information and don't bring it to the rest of the crew, your mistake in the eyes of the crew is bigger than the one the crew is about to make.

◆

Problems during a football game can be resolved if properly defined with good information. Someone on the crew has the missing information, almost always, to solve the problem.

◆

It is quite unfair to make judgments about other officials unless there is compassion.

◆

Every crew has baggage. The more baggage that is checked at the pregame, the less chance for excess during the game.

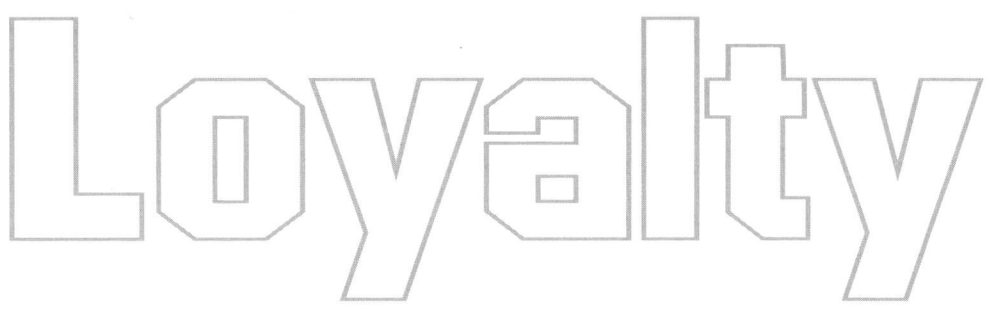

Loyalty

Any member of the crew can make a mistake, but he hasn't failed until he starts blaming members of his crew.

◆

Crews need confidentiality, so keep crew leaks in the locker room urinal.

◆

Competition within the crew brings out the best in the individual and the absolute worst between crews.

◆

Every situation in a football game that requires an official interpretation contains within the problem the seeds for its own solution.

◆

A good crew is like a good ship; everyone should be able to take the helm, or in football, at least be able to work three different positions.

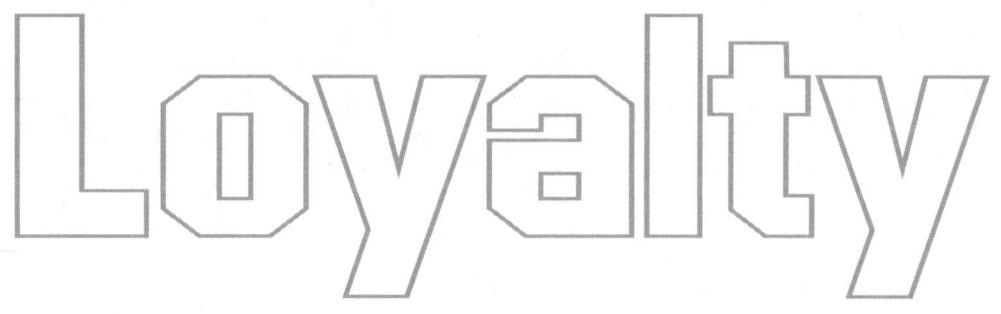

Individual members of a crew promoted to the next level of officiating are usually promoted because of the work of the entire crew.

◆

If you are going to be wrong five times during a football game, be wrong three times for poor mechanics, two times for judgment and zero times for rule interpretations, then get better each week for five weeks.

◆

Not helping members of your own crew to improve is like burning down your home to get rid of a rat.

◆

When officials get into a rut, they need to realize that the depth of the sides could be a grave.

◆

Changing talent to ability is the key to a referee successfully making a good crew into great crew.

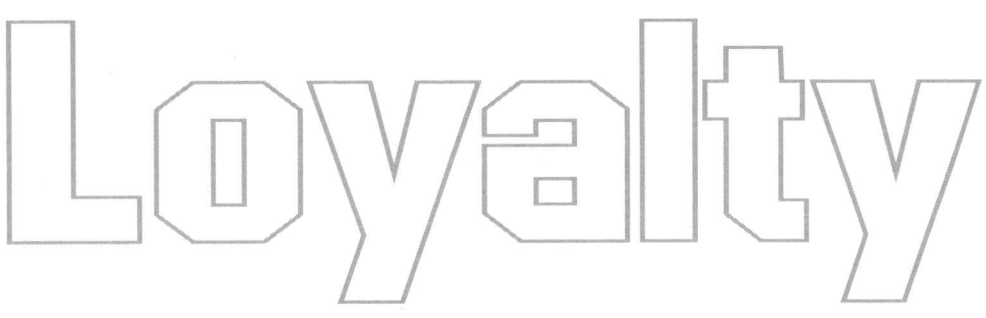

Loyalty

In the confusion of a difficult situation on the field, when the obstacles and options appear overwhelming, simply return to your most basic assumption about the play and follow your instincts.

◆

The best crews simply find ways of doing the common routine parts of a football game better than anyone else.

◆

The best referees take genuine joy and celebration in the success and advancement of each crew member.

◆

Don't tell me after the game about a mistake we could have corrected on the field. Hindsight is an exact science, but a poor substitution for on-the-field crew communication.

◆

The difference between a good game and a great game, is just a little extra effort by the crew, individually and collectively.

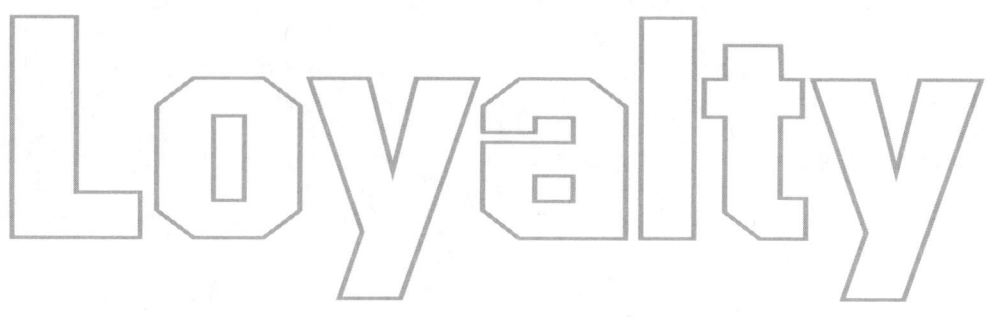

Loyalty

The best measure of self-evaluation for an official, is simply how much better he has made his crew.

◆

When the light simply goes out on the field for an official, but a crew member blows a new flame to rekindle the official, everybody wins.

◆

The chemistry of the referee to the crew is very important, as everyone in the crew needs to know what he stands for, as well as what he won't stand for.

◆

The best referees find the ability to be a bridge to each of their crew members.

◆

A good referee will convince his crew that self interest is not as important as crew interest.

◆

When everyone on the crew agrees on everything all the time, the crew needs a new member or two.

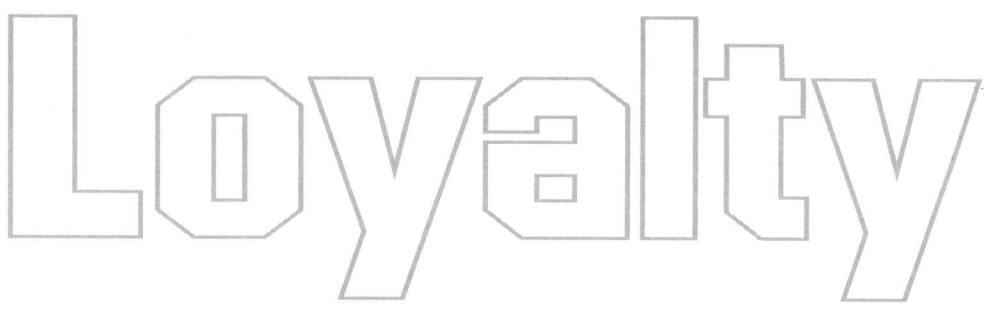

Loyalty

The harmony of a great crew working together is not when everyone is singing the same note.

◆

Some football crews confuse the poor leadership of their referee with destiny. It becomes self-fulfilling.

◆

Mistakes in a football game are going to occur. The very best that you can do for a crew member is to correct a mistake that is about to be made that would have created an advantage for a team.

◆

When a crew works hard during the week preparing for the game, has a great pregame, and then says, "Good game everyone. We must be lucky." It is really hard to detect luck because it looks like they earned it.

◆

Why do some crews have all the luck? Maybe they have the luck of having the talent.

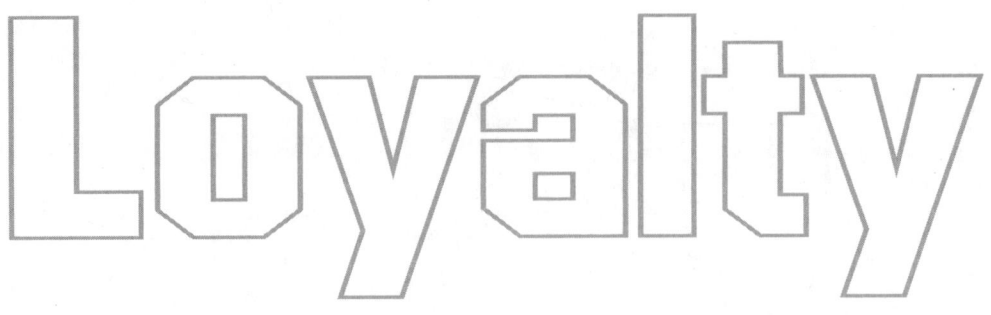

Loyalty

The strength in the crew concept is that it allows extraordinary potential with ordinary officials.

◆

After the play when the flag or flags are down, getting the facts is the key to a good decision. Almost every mistake we make, individually or as a crew, came because we didn't take the time or drive hard enough to get the facts.

◆

If your crew is full of willing officials, find out which are willing to work a great game, and which are willing to let others…

◆

Go out as seven; come back as seven. Unity gives your crew strength.

◆

The best crews have harmony, but on the field they work together as a melody.

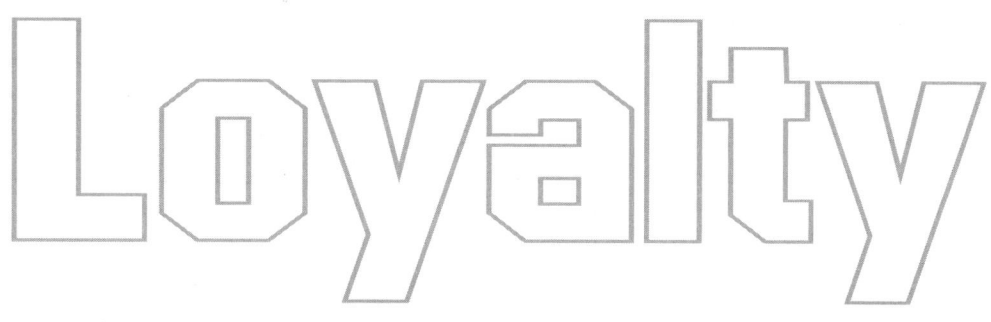

Loyalty

A good test about the character of an official is what he says about the rest of his crew, which is actually more important than what his crew says about him.

◆

The absolute toughest situation on the field for your crew to resolve will be much easier if you take a deep breath and look at it as if it is an opportunity.

◆

If some of the crew creates a hole in coverage, communication or mechanics, they create a problem for the whole crew.

◆

In order to have a great crew, each official must put his crew ahead of his personal goals and bowl aspirations.

◆

The class crew in the conference has an invisible quality which commands respect rather than attempting to demand it.

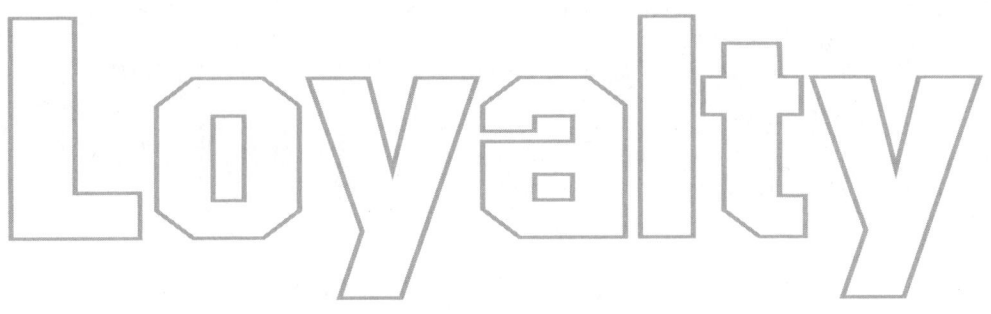

Loyalty

If you have your choice in a crew to be successful or to be of value, choose value.

---◆---

A successful officiating crew divides all of the task and doubles the crew's success.

---◆---

A referee can't compromise his principles, but he can coordinate tactics to preserve unity within the crew.

---◆---

It is great for a referee to have ability — A greater gift is his ability to improve the ability and work ethic of his crew.

---◆---

The best way to not be jealous of other crews is to take pride in your crew.

---◆---

Don't let special crew rules be a fashionable substitute for approved mechanics.

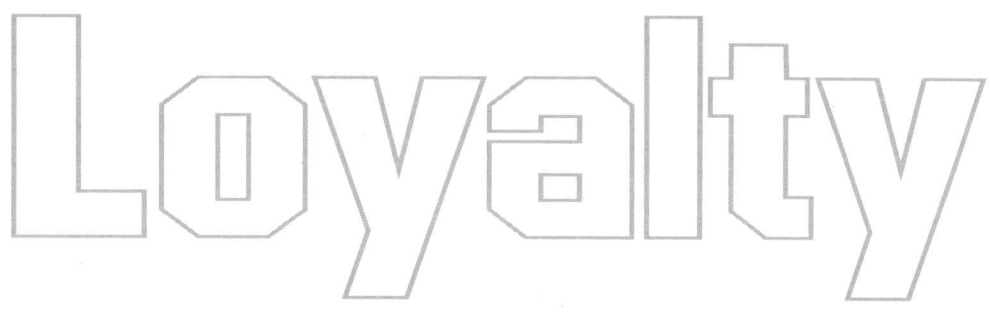

Loyalty

Some games for a crew are like seven balloons (officials) dancing on a field of pins, just waiting to explode. Somehow, the good ones defuse the situation.

♦

A successful football crew: comes together, stays together, works together.

♦

A comedy of errors can be a tragedy to the crew.

♦

Every crew needs a brakeman, but you do not want him to have the brakes on all of the time.

♦

Beware of the crew member who smiles when someone makes a mistake, as it simply means he has found someone to blame it on.

♦

Luck is not as important to the very best crews.

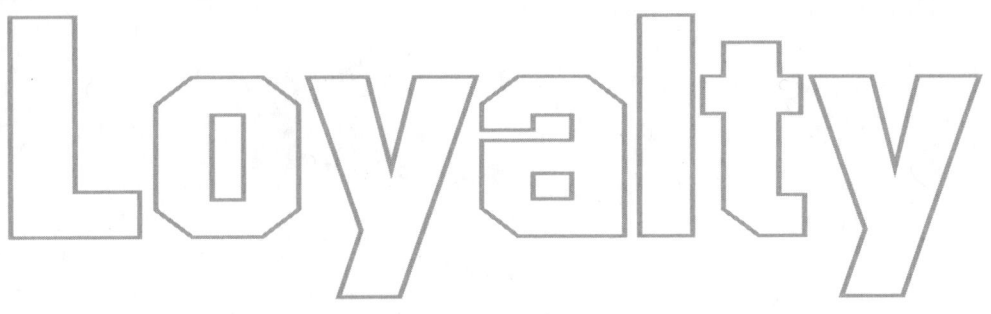

Loyalty

If your crew has worked a terribly bad game, and you can't figure out who to blame, you are.

◆

The strength of the best crews often increases in proportion to the obstacles which are given during the game.

◆

When you help another official, you have doubled the learning.

◆

One of the best ways for some officials to get up for a game is to get a crew member up for the game.

◆

Seven great officials do not equal a great crew.

◆

Everyone on the crew could be somebody else's lunch. Make sure you go out as seven and come back to the locker room as seven officials.

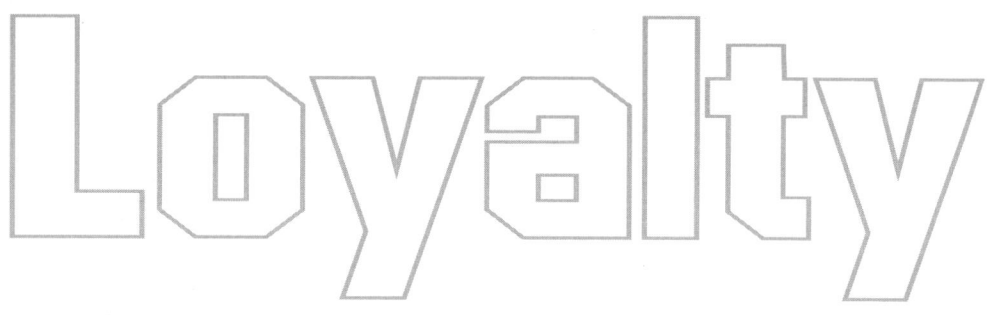

Loyalty

One good head in a crew conference is much better than 14 strong hands.

Few things help a crew more than to place responsibility upon each member. Let them know that you trust and depend on them to officiate as a crew better.

It is okay to be on top of the heap; just remember that you are still part of the heap.

The corporate official is an official looking for individual profit with no regard for crew responsibility.

It is said that sticks in a bundle are unbreakable. The same is true for a crew that doesn't bend. It can sustain the pressure of 80,000 fans and ESPN.

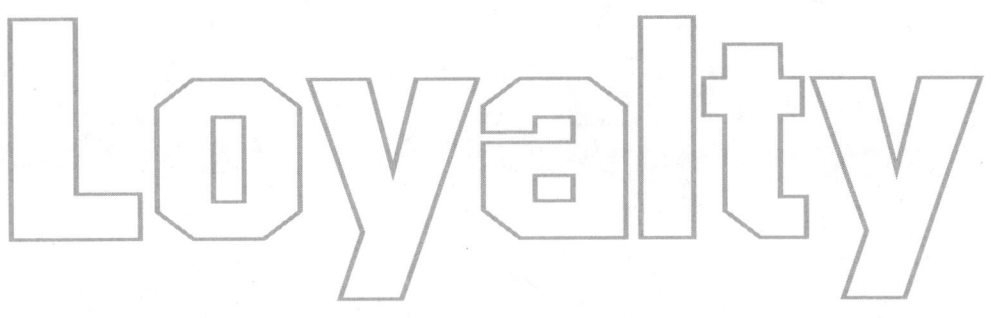
Loyalty

If a crew or individual looks at the biggest mistakes made in a game, they will find that most start with false pride.

———◆———

Just as when your neighbor's wall catches on fire, you have the responsibility to put water on the situation and bail your officiating partner out when you can.

———◆———

A crew's chance to officiate a successful or difficult game, shrinks or expands in proportion to the courage of the crew.

———◆———

When dealing with a difficult situation, good officials find stepping stones; poor officials use stumbling blocks.

———◆———

During an emotional crew conference, it may be easy to be critical, but the real test is to come up with a constructive solution to the problem.

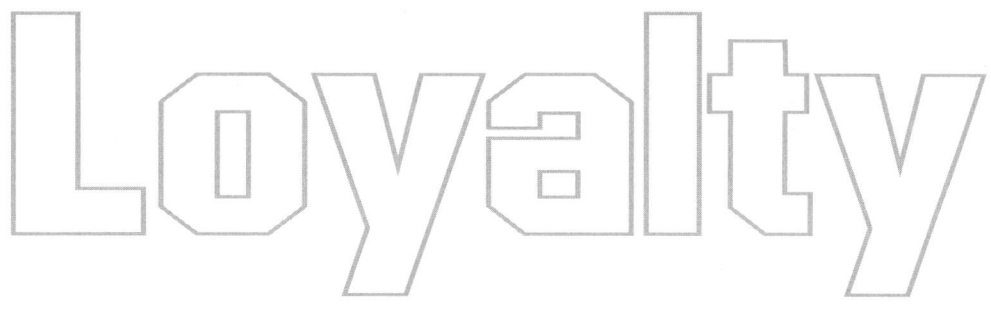

Loyalty

Not all members of the crew have received their training and experience from the same ship, but on game day they are all in the same boat.

◆

If you will only be satisfied with the "perfect crew," you are clueless and will soon be crewless.

◆

Fill a place on the crew, not a space.

◆

Crew jealousy is contagious and is nothing more than poison envy.

Section 8

Mechanics

Colorado concentration.

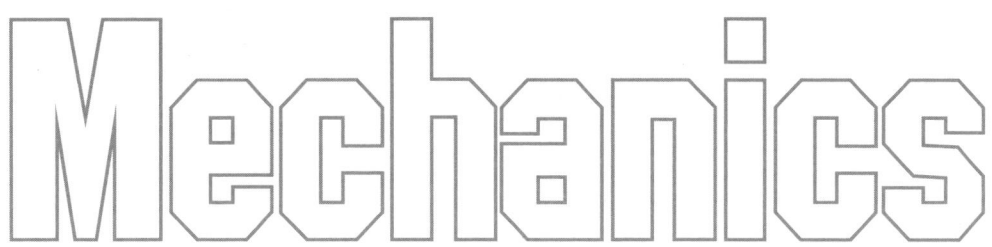

Mechanics

This section may be the least interesting to the "non-football" fan, as it does point out some of the technical concerns that can surface when a crew or individual decides during a game to do his "own thing." Still it is not unlike problems faced in the business world, but possibly a little technical for the reader with no interest in football. But I must add, if you have an interest in football, you can create some good conversation with any sports official.

    Some officials prepare for the play, recognize their keys, and dodge their responsibility to officiate the play.

——◆——

    A referee trying to change the mechanics of his crew is like moving a cemetery. Until you have actually tried it, you will never realize how many dead friends you have.

——◆——

    Failing on each down to communicate to at least one other official, down/distance is about the same as winking at a pretty girl in a dark closet. You know what you are doing, but no one else does.

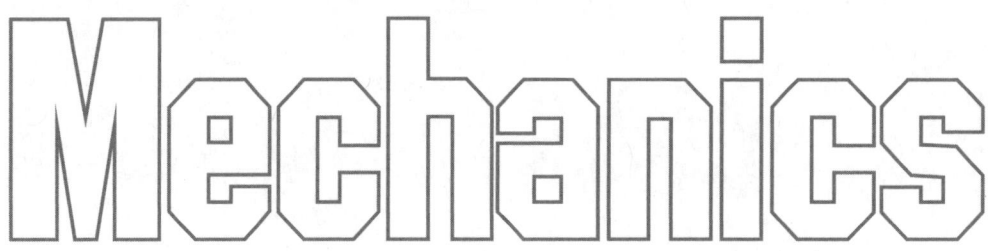

Mechanics

Good mechanics are something you do without thinking which gives you time to see the play without interruptions.

◆

Even in sports officiating, when good mechanics are carried to an excess, they are not effective or appreciated.

◆

Bad mechanics in officiating cannot be overcome by repetition. They can only be overcome by developing good mechanics.

◆

It is easier to prevent "bad mechanics" than to break them.

◆

Poor mechanics can sometimes be the secret that you don't know you are keeping.

◆

The lack of a good pre-snap routine is a comfortable but deadly disease.

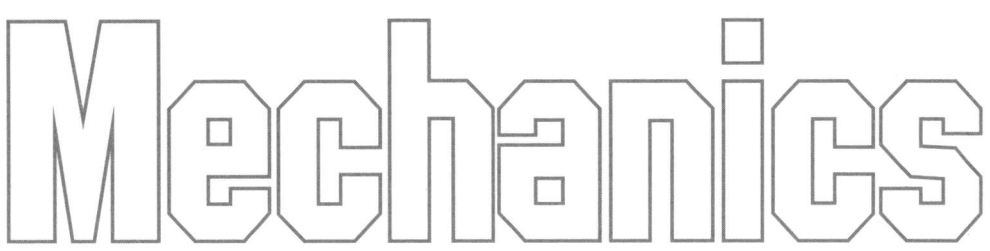

Mechanics

Officials are divided into three classes: those who read and remember, those who read and forget, and those who read and apply every sentence they read on every snap, and never understand the game.

―――◆―――

Useless mechanics will weaken the flow of the game.

―――◆―――

Anyone who has ever made the claim of officiating a game and making no mistakes has never watched all of their keys from the first kick-off through the first punt in the game. Sorry, but mistakes were made.

―――◆―――

You can't count on your judgment when your concentration is not strong.

―――◆―――

Before the snap, don't waste time judging your previous mistake. Refocus, concentrate and get better.

Mechanics

Bad habits and bad mechanics are first cobwebs; then they become cables.

―◆―

Check your keys and your understanding of the game if what is anticipated never happens and what you least expect generally happens.

―◆―

You can't depend on your eyes when your keys are out of focus.

―◆―

Mechanics and keys are great routines to help you avoid mistakes. Experience enables you to sometimes recognize a mistake when you are about ready to make it again.

―◆―

Far too often in football associations or crews, officials develop their own "special mechanics" — Mechanizitis;" which when observed by those knowledgeable of the game, looks like a spastic colon.

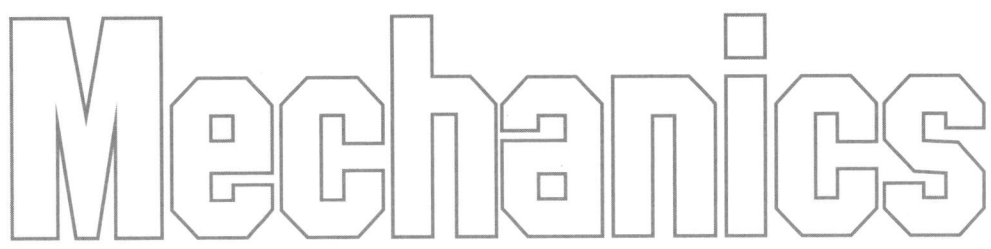

One of the very best and quickest ways to bail out a fellow official is through eye contact — Eye contact transcends speech — Use it.

———◆———

Good habits (mechanics) reduce bad mistakes.

———◆———

The best officials use their best mechanics even when no one is watching.

———◆———

Missing your pre-snap keys is an early warning system to unfolding mis-calculations.

———◆———

After you have blown an inadvertent whistle, "You can't hide under the astro turf." (Virgil Deering, Retired Big 8) Come forward, explain to the referee, and be better the remainder of the game.

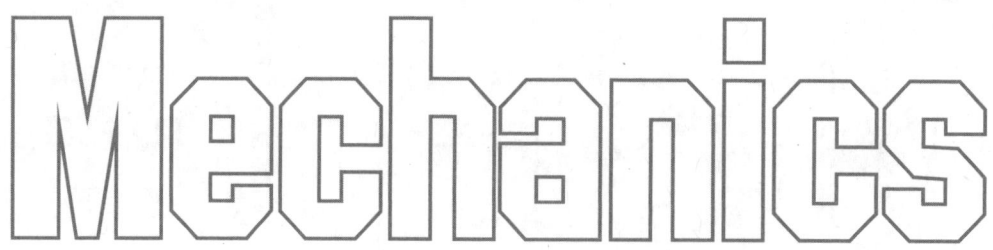

Eye contact can do more, quicker, than two hands or two feet.

◆

Over-running a play has the same effectiveness in a football game as the speed of a runaway horse.

◆

Keep the whistle out of your mouth…He who hesitates is many times saved.

◆

When you lose passion for doing your best, lose concentration and "keys" for the next snap, and are not looking forward to the next game, but one "down-the-line," your days are numbered.

◆

See the play, make the call. Use your eyes for two seconds after a tight play — You can still use an eraser, the whistle is like permanent ink.

◆

Mechanics: The art of doing something well and not having to think about it.

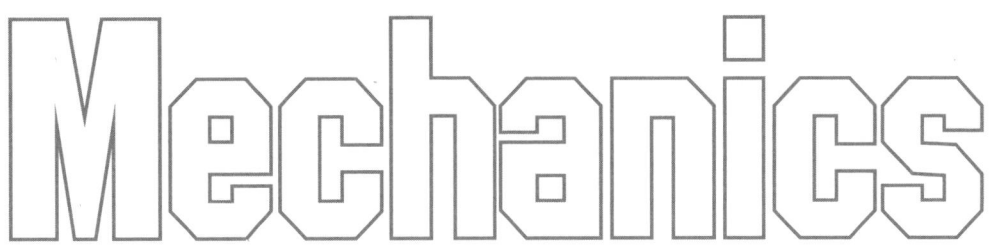

Mechanics

If you have to think about the mechanics involved in officiating the game, you are NOT well prepared.

◆

Poor mechanics are a species of idleness and laziness.

◆

Let the colors uniforms separate before you do your laundry with ball mechanics.

◆

A player with "a brick in his hand," or an opponent "counting change," requires presence and voice as a foul is about to occur.

◆

If you are "watching the game" and not "seeing the play" through your keys, don't throw your flag. Buy a ticket, get some popcorn and enjoy the game.

◆

"See the play, make the call" — This is a very good mechanic especially if you have a photographic memory. Just make sure you have film in the camera.

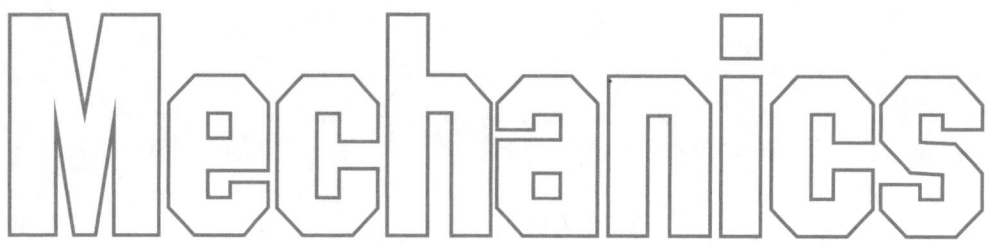

Mechanics

Some officials are so broke they can't pay attention to their keys in officiating the game.

―◆―

If you make a mistake, refocus, pick up your "key/mechanics" and move on.

―◆―

Good officiating mechanics are sometimes hard to form but easy to live with; while bad mechanics are easy to form, but hard to live by.

―◆―

The only way to get rid of bad officiating habits is to acquire good habits contradictory to bad habits.

―◆―

In officiating, try to make adjustments and corrections while things are going well in the game rather than waiting until things are going poorly.

―◆―

Many mistakes in officiating are made by a first "quick" response — Don't just do something — Stand there, process, then do something.

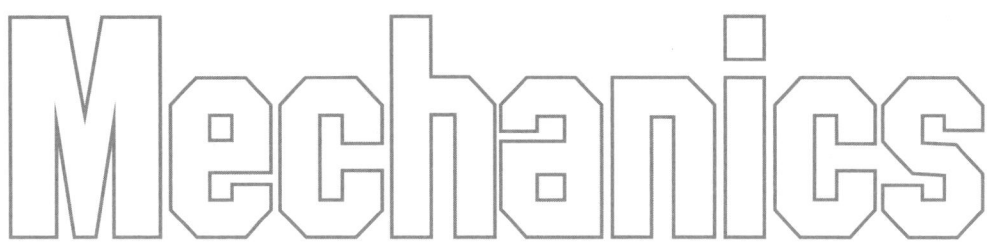

Direct involvement in officiating decreases in direct proportion to an official's distance from the play.

◆

"Controlling the line of scrimmage" is a great deodorant to a game with a chance to "stink."

◆

See the ball! Look for help! Make the call!

◆

Eye contact reduces the chance of error 20-20. (20 out of 20 times you will get the call correct with eye contact from another official.)

◆

Good signals are actually a visual telegram to coaches, players, fans and even announcers, to keep them from trying to tell their own story.

◆

If you have prepared yourself to observe the play, the correct interpretation is much easier to make.

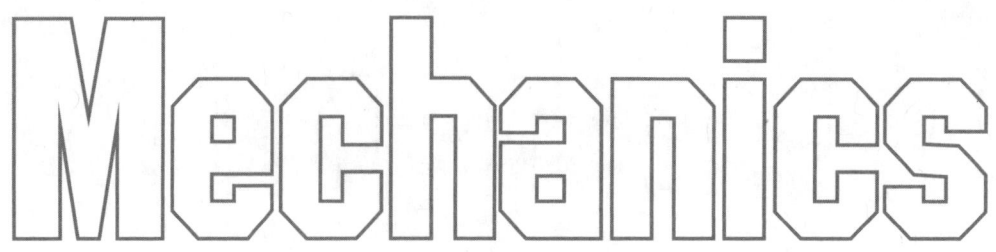

It is sometimes a very short step between a well officiated game and a poor one. The step is usually mechanic, routine, gesture, eye contact or a single word. Little things are important.

———◆———

It is better not to see the foul at all than to guess wrong.

———◆———

Too much "scrubbing" and too many flags take the life out of things and games.

———◆———

Luck is increased by paying close attention to details.

———◆———

If you over-run your position on the field, you are moving forward twice the speed of "sight" and half the speed of "sense."

———◆———

We make our habits (mechanics) good or bad; then our habits make us.

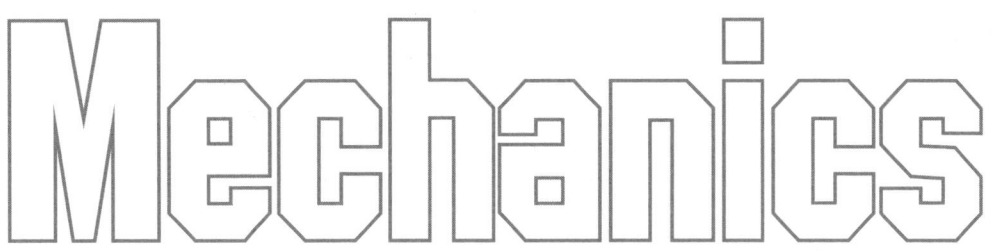

Mechanics

Most officiating problems are not caused by inability, but because of inconsistency.

———◆———

Not following the keys, rituals, or mechanics is a quality that allows poor officials to follow a path of least persistence.

———◆———

It is possible to have good vision on the field and still have "I" trouble.

———◆———

Poor officials develop little bad habits (mechanics) that eventually become too strong to break.

NU/KSU two of the three teams on the field. Our goal should always be to have a "better game as a crew than the two on the line-of-scrimmage."

Section 9
Philosophy

Over 40 years of Education Administration, Principal of the Year, Missouri, 1995.

Philosophy

This is the largest and most random section of the book. You will find this section entertaining to read. This material is simply a collection of general statements about officiating and life that apply to most other sections of this book in a more general manner.

At some point in your officiating career you will have a play or situation in which you will choose to protect your reputation or to make the right decision. The choice at the time may be very difficult, but those officials with a great career always make the right decision and in the end have enhanced their reputation.

———◆———

If your officiating philosophy is that you are not going to make anyone mad, then you are ultimately seeking the lowest common denominator of officiating achievement.

———◆———

Getting even "evening them up," throws an athletic contest out of balance with its natural flow.

Philosophy

Officiate every game like it could be your last, and one day you will be correct.

◆

Be as fully prepared for the dull game as you are for the great game, or you won't be prepared for the dull game that becomes a great game.

◆

The most successful officials have the capacity to move from a mistake to the next play without any loss of enthusiasm.

◆

If you let the conditions of a football game stop you from officiating a good game, they will always stop you.

◆

Not believing in momentum is like not believing in gravity. Although neither can be seen, they both can be felt. Develop your own momentum and understand the momentum of the game.

Philosophy

An official "surprised" by a play on the field is "half-beaten."

---◆---

Failure is the condiment that gives a "successful" officiated game a special reward.

---◆---

Some of the toughest games to officiate are successful not because of the strength of the crew, but simply perseverance to be the best of three teams on the field.

---◆---

If you have enthusiasm to officiate and truly look forward to each game, your chances of a long and successful career have been greatly increased.

---◆---

Ask yourself as an official, is it the "easiest" decision or is it the "right" decision to make?

Philosophy

If you can be right 147 out of 150 football plays, no one remembers. But if you are wrong three out of 150 plays, no one forgets.

◆

Some young officials following their dad's footsteps inherit some good instincts, but in time they overcome them.

◆

Every game has an opportunity for a ridiculous and unnecessary penalty. If you look for it, you can find it.

◆

The best things in life are not "things" or "games" — But people and experiences.

◆

Sometimes officials can get "caught" in damaging consequences outside of their control. There are painful situations where officials have been ruined by their knowledge and fired for their courage.

Philosophy

It is not uncommon in a great game between two evenly matched teams to have disorderliness. The key is to establish a good fair "flow" to this type of game.

◆

Part of getting over the fact that you officiated a game in which there were five downs in a series is to know that you will never completely get over it.

◆

Don't force the game to be longer than it wants to be.

◆

The history of officiating: There comes a time when the rebellious young officials take their turn as experienced officials, against whom the next wave of rookies can rebel.

◆

Football stadiums are paved with the bones of officials with no courage to see the play and make the call.

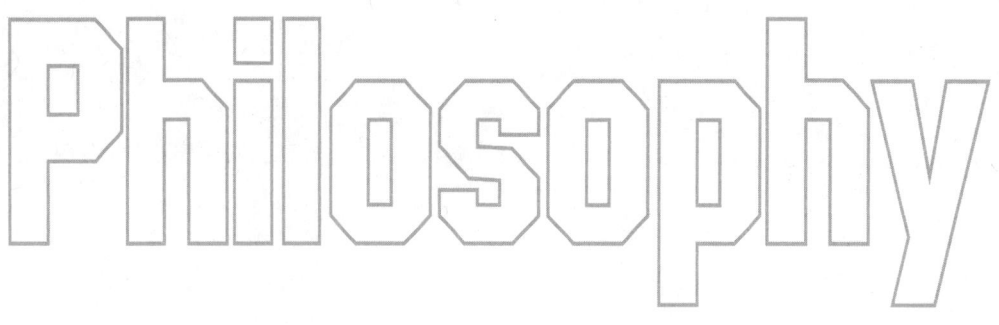

Philosophy

To hesitate and be right has a career advantage over being quick and wrong.

———◆———

You will achieve your goal much quicker and more professionally if you work, not to be better than everyone else at your position, but to simply improve yourself each game.

———◆———

Simplify complicated situations in an emotional game.

———◆———

They don't sell tickets to last week's game. Move on and improve.

———◆———

In the last quarter of a well-officiated football game, endurance is simply patience and focus concentrated.

———◆———

You can plan and prepare and still run into plain old "dumb luck." It is what you do after this happens that separates officials.

Philosophy

If you are going to try to make a simple play difficult to officiate, try to pick an easy one.

◆

The measure of success in an officiating career is not whether you have a tough season, but whether you have the same problems the next season.

◆

It is easy for officials to look good if there are no possibilities for bad options.

◆

Tough games reveal the quality and character of an official — Easy games to officiate conceal a lot of things.

◆

Good officials know they are "good." Poor officials "pretend" they are good.

◆

If you are not a little nervous before the first kick-off, you have probably not set expectations high enough for yourself.

Philosophy

Pride in what you do as an official is a personal commitment, but it is your attitude that separates excellence from mediocre officiating.

◆

You either plan to work a great game, or you plan not to work a bad game. This is the key difference between success and mediocrity.

◆

No official, who has ever given his best each game, has ever had regrets about his career; regardless of the level at which he officiated.

◆

Officiating is a balance between preventable acts and appropriate reaction.

◆

The official you need to be most concerned about, at your position, is the one behind the one in front of you.

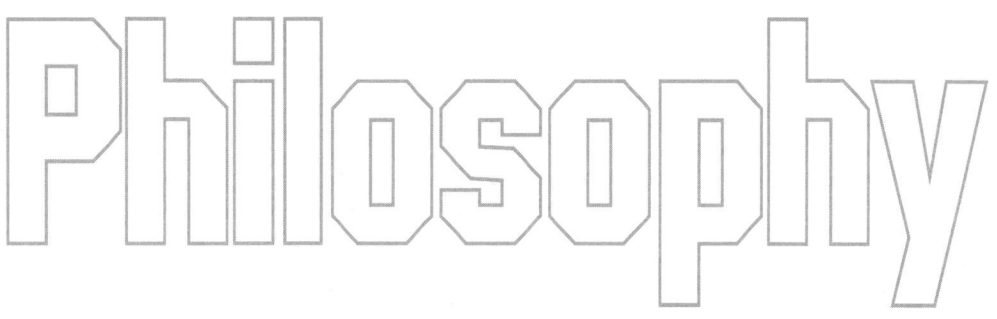

Philosophy

Officiating is comfortable when you know the rules and easy when you understand the game.

◆

Problems in officiating a football game are problematic. The problem becomes the problem when we focus on WHY we are having problems instead of solving the problem on the field.

◆

Throw your flag or leave it in your pocket, but spare all of us the gutless act of indifference.

◆

There are two ways of meeting difficulties during a game: You alter the difficulties or you alter yourself.

◆

No one likes to fail, so think of it as time-released success.

◆

Before you are "over-the-hill", try spending a little time at the top and then stop before the slide.

Don't let small things have big shadows.

———◆———

The quality of a person's life is in direct proportion to their commitment to excellence, regardless of there chosen field of endeavor. (Vince Lombardi)

———◆———

When the game loses its flow and is out of sync, find a way to enjoy the scenery as you work through the detour.

———◆———

If you are not going to give it your best each snap, why are you doing it all?

———◆———

When the game is tough, it is not the situation but your REACTION to the situation.

———◆———

The only real mistake from a mistake in a football game is if nothing is learned.

Philosophy

Some mistakes we bring upon ourselves, and others are completely beyond our control. But no matter what happens to us on the field, we always have some control over what we do about it.

◆

A football game is a series of moments. Officiate each, one at a time, in order to succeed.

◆

There is no distance on earth farther away than last week's game. Good or bad, get over it and be better next week.

◆

The way to approach a difficult and complex situation is to try to look at it as an opportunity to get this one right. It is simply disguised opportunity.

◆

Get the game started right and on time. A good beginning sets up a good ending.

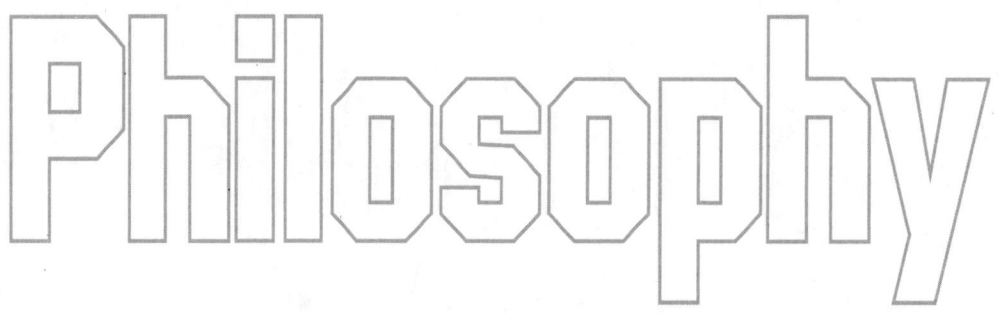

Games create different situations. Everything depends upon circumstances, and you must sail according to the wind.

◆

The best reward for officiating a great game is to simply have done it.

◆

Take time to enjoy the game when you don't even have time for it; you will be more relaxed and make better decisions.

◆

Most well-officiated football games are not a matter of chance, but simply a matter of choice.

◆

Nothing erases unpleasant situations more effectively than conscious concentration on a positive situation that occurs during the game.

◆

One measure of a successful, experienced official is to know when to kiss ass, kick or save ass!

Philosophy

The approach to resolving a multiple foul-situation is to make stepping stones out of stumbling blocks.

◆

There is a big difference in reaching your goal to become a major college official and getting better each year. One is terminal, and the other is a long, successful career.

◆

A well-officiated football game is not a matter of milestones, but rather the game is made up of moments.

◆

How to improve as an official: 1). Admit it when you are wrong. 2). Be smart enough to profit from your errors. 3). Be strong enough to make corrections.

◆

In the case of the inadvertent whistle, the unvarnished truth is always better than the best-dressed lie.

Philosophy

There are two games that you should not worry about, your last one and your next one.

———◆———

What has working the very toughest game of your career just done for you? It simply made the next one that will be even tougher, easier. The road of experience is long, but shorter the second time.

———◆———

Every game has a play that you "passed on" and could have thrown a flag. In fact, you may have missed the call. Good officials have this image out of their mind before the next snap, remembering to make the most of what you can, and the least of what has passed.

———◆———

Don't justify a mistake; learn from it.

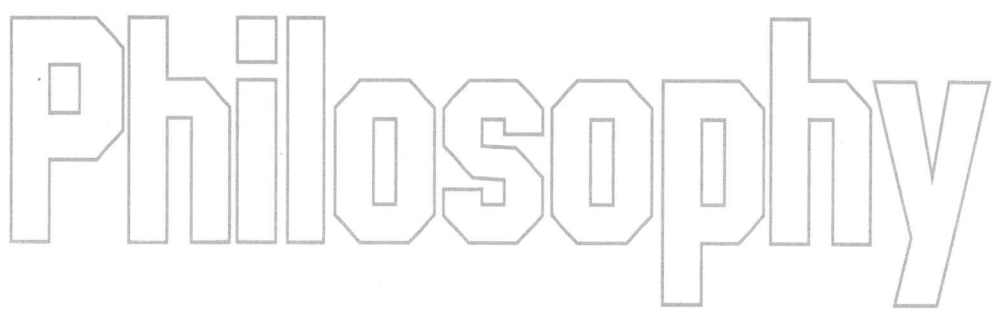

Philosophy

About the time an official believes there can be no serious consequences, from "little things" in a football game, something BIG develops from a "little thing," and we realize that there are no little things.

◆

The only thing some tough games measure is your patience.

◆

To see a foul and not make the call is an officiating mistake. But to not give thought to what has been seen and call a foul is even a more serious mistake.

◆

The real test of character in an official is how he handles himself and the situation after he makes a mistake.

◆

Officiating a good football game is 75% preparation and 25% adjustment.

Philosophy

Have 20/20 vision inside the lines and have a hearing loss outside the lines.

◆

The difficult part of becoming a major-college official and moving up the ladder is getting through the crowd at the bottom.

◆

"Everybody's got a plan until he gets hit." (Mike Tyson)

◆

"It's what you do with your plan when things come apart that makes you a good official." Dave Laurie, Retired Kansas State University Professor.

◆

Breaks balance out. The sun don't shine on the same ol' dog's ass every day. (Darrell Royal)

◆

Compromise the small things, and get all of the big things right.

Philosophy

"The eyes see only what the mind is prepared to digest." (Butch Clark, Big 8)

---◆---

Officials see only what they are prepared to see.

---◆---

"You can learn a lot by just watching." (Yogi Berra)

---◆---

Don't major on the minors.

---◆---

The potential difference in officiating a good and poor football game is what is between the talents and expectations.

---◆---

Age is a high price to pay for experience…Get better each game, and don't repeat mistakes.

Philosophy

Every morning in Africa, a gazelle wakes up. It knows it must run faster than the fastest lion or it will be killed. Every morning, a lion wakes up. It knows it must outrun the slowest gazelle or it will starve to death. So it doesn't matter whether you are a lion or a gazelle, when the sun comes up, you'd better be running. (George Allen, Washington Redskins.)

◆

Every ball carrier is a potential fumbler. (Bruce Finlayson, Big 8 Supervisor, retired.)

◆

There is nothing the rookie official can't do that the No. 1 rated official in America can't do… Without 10 years experience.

◆

The secret of the joy in officiating is contained in the excellence. To know how to do something well and enjoy it is the secret.

Even after the worst five minutes of game-stopping miscues, refocus because the game goes on.

◆

The supreme goal in officiating a great football game is to blur the line between work and fun.

◆

Never mistake movement for hustle.

◆

Think positive. Some officials think negative, predict their failures and then do their best to live up to their own prophecies.

◆

Football is a game played by imperfect players, coached by imperfect coaches, and officiated by imperfect officials. Officiating is as much a part of the game as running, blocking and tackling. Mistaken decisions will even out as long as the officials are men of integrity, which is the only thing that really matters. (Bruce Finlayson, Big 8 Supervisor, retired)

Philosophy

Chance, good luck and good bounces favor the best prepared.

―◆―

An official who is waiting and not working toward becoming a major-college official, should keep in mind this Chinese proverb: "He who waits for a roast duck to fly into his mouth, must wait a very, very long time."

―◆―

Sitting in the stands on Saturday afternoon, the daughter of an official soon learns several names she never knew her father had. (Tracy Laurie, daughter of Big 8/12 official, Phil Laurie.)

―◆―

A snake will still bite you even if you call it Mr. Snake. An inadvertent whistle will still cause problems even if you apologize.

Philosophy

To work a great football game don't take your eyes off your goal. But if you are going to accomplish your goal, you are going to have to take your eyes off the ball most of the time.

◆

An inadvertent whistle is as irrevocable as a short hair cut.

◆

Why do some crews have all the luck? Maybe they have the luck of having the talent.

◆

It is usually better to pass on a rule you are not sure of, than misapply a rule that you thought was correct.

◆

Anyone too busy to reflect on his last game is too busy to improve.

Philosophy

Life is simpler when you plow around the stump. The same is true with a situation you can't control during a football game. Don't dig a hole if it is not necessary.

◆

When things are confusing, an ounce of patience is worth a pound of brains.

◆

Worrying about the play you missed is like sitting in a rocking chair. It will give you something to do, you won't go anywhere, and more importantly… You just missed the next play.

◆

When officials begin to talk about retirement, they probably already have.

◆

Great officials have their limitations, but stupid officials have no boundaries.

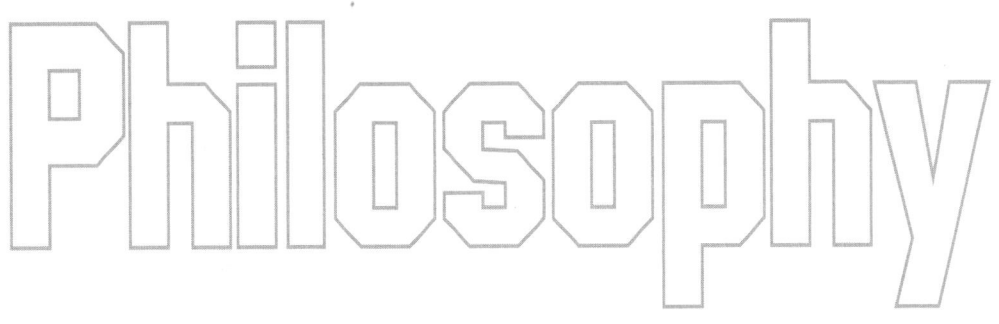

Philosophy

Mediocre officials recognize their level and work hard to stay there. Those with talent work to improve.

Officials who fail fall into two categories: Those who thought about it and never followed through, and those who officiated but never gave any thought to the game.

Some officials hesitate and make mistakes because they feel inferior. The best ones are busy making mistakes and becoming superior officials.

The official who always excuses himself, accuses himself.

If you have the ability to carry a football game to the perception of "simplicity in flow," it has a feel of excellence.

Philosophy

No official is really lost at his position. He is easily found, but just didn't belong.

What you don't see with your eyes, don't invent with your flag.

"You can't shoot rabbits off a galloping horse." (Mike Weir, Big 8/12, NFL)

"Don't worry about the fly crap in the pepper." (Terry Porter, Big 8/12 official).

If you make every game a life and death proposition, for one thing, you'll be dead a lot. (Dean Smith, North Carolina.)

The only way to describe the feeling of having an inadvertent whistle is to realize, after you have blown your whistle, the fearsome desire to be lonesome.

Philosophy

Hustle, get in the film.

♦

Be a "dead ball" official; watch the fringes.

♦

"Do what brung you here." (Kent Houck, Big 8 official, Retired)

♦

Hustle under control.

♦

Anticipate the play and not the call.

♦

A well-dressed official wears a uniform that no one notices.

♦

"Let the foul come to you; don't go looking for it." (Artie Palk, Big 8 Official, Retired)

Philosophy

An official is like a tea bag; you can't tell how good he is until you put him in hot water.

◆

"Talk" to the pile.

◆

People who complain about the way the ball bounces are usually the ones who have dropped it.

◆

When the one great scorer goes to put an official in his book, it doesn't matter how you called the game, but how did you make it look. (Phil Laurie, Big 8/12)

◆

A well-officiated football game is simply triumph over chaos.

◆

Officials with integrity and lack of knowledge of rules are simply well-intended, poor officials. Book officials without integrity should be removed from officiating.

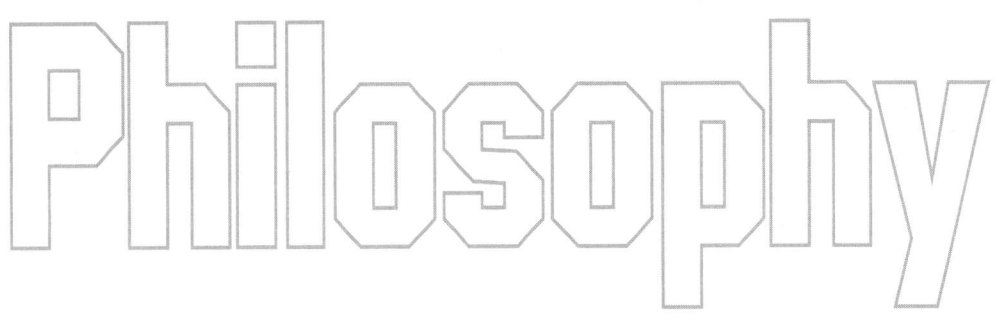

Philosophy

When we have worked ourselves into a difficult situation, it is often because we have given the play that we could have avoided, a chance to beat us.

◆

The game of football has a set of rules. Integrity has no need for rules.

◆

There is no such thing as a "perfectly officiated game." Perfection is a moving target; adjustment is the key to a great game.

◆

Perfection in officiating is misleading because the pursuit of it often impedes improvement.

◆

Visualizing the perfect play, the perfect quarter, half or game, allows the official to have constant optimism, as well as, a strong multiplier for things to come.

Philosophy

The only way to describe the feeling of an inadvertent whistle is to be dead among the living. (usually 50,000 fans).

―◆―

I never try for a game to be the best I have ever worked; I just want the next one to be better than the last one.

―◆―

Go out as seven , come back as seven, come back tired. (physically and emotionally.) (Bill Jennings, Big 8, retired.)

―◆―

Extreme interpretation of a rule usually means extreme unfair application — Avoid extremes in officiating.

―◆―

Keep the game moving — Some officials make nothing happen very slowly.

Philosophy

Sometimes when you "throw" your flag against the home team, and the entire crowd roars as you bring back a touchdown, and you feel everyone in the stadium is against you, keep in mind that there are always a few tourists from a foreign country thinking they are at a soccer match who are neutral or don't give a damn.

◆

Separate "colors" (players from different teams) before retrieving a ball or tending to other "details."

◆

During the national anthem, the object is not to get rid of the butterflies, but to get them to fly in formation.

◆

There is danger in over-officiating (calling it too close), but there is more concern by being blindly conservative and calling no fouls when they are "there."

Philosophy

If your "dream" is to become a major college football official, you must wake up.

◆

Consistent officiating is being fair and honest. It is not having the same number of fouls called on each team.

◆

How do you approach a problem on the field? Stumbling block or stepping stone?

◆

A big head is a big load for a crew to carry.

◆

Don't get trapped into 120 consecutive well-officiated plays and then lose the opportunity to use common sense to keep a good "flow" to the game.

◆

Some officials are so ill-prepared that when the "opportunity knocks," they are deaf to the knock.

Philosophy

To believe two teams are so bad, or so unequal in talent, and therefore impossible to officiate, is to make it so.

◆

Every difficult situation that occurs on the football field presents two very clear directions: 1). An opportunity for you to do your best. 2). A chance to show that you can fail. If 90% of officiating is mental, is there any question what your attitude should be when placed in this situation?

◆

Sometimes you just have to laugh at yourself. He who laughs — last. (Your career is too short to take everything too seriously.)

◆

Officiating the perfect game isn't everything, but doing your best work is.

◆

Things turn out best for crews who make the best of the way things turn out.

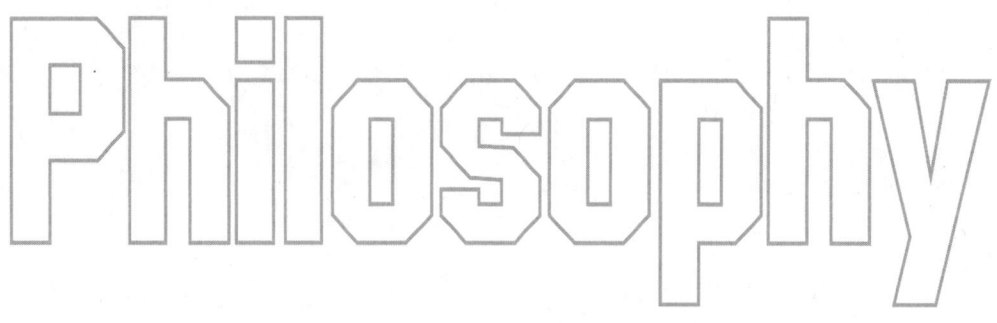

Philosophy

The greatest legacy a retiring official can leave the game is being perceived as a man of integrity.

―◆―

After a tough game, never ruin an apology with an excuse.

―◆―

Behind every great official in the conference, there will always be others just as good or even better waiting their turn to take your place.

―◆―

Good officials don't stumble over the same stone twice.

―◆―

If you and your crew have done their best in a poorly played game, what else is there? Move on!

―◆―

With only a few exceptions, a well-officiated football game is not a matter of chance, but a choice. It is not something that a crew wishes for, but it is something that they all work to attain.

Philosophy

Patience in a difficult situation can allow wisdom to surface.

Young, energetic and eager officials should not reach earlier than necessary or farther than they can grasp.

Practice is the very best teacher of officiating the game of football. "Get the snaps" and experience the game if you wish to become a "censored" "seasoned" effective official.

The reward for a successful officiating is the opportunity to continue to do something that many would like to do in your place.

Sometimes the opportunity that you are looking for in a game or even your career can be disguised in the form of misfortune or a temporary defeat.

Art and the rule book have this in common. You must draw a line somewhere, and in officiating, the most difficult part is to be consistent.

◆

A sense of fairness is the moral glue to each official, and the tough part is that it is subject to constant stress.

◆

"Passing" on a tough, important and difficult call may have been seen as a great call. Learn from this experience. If it was really "cold feet" that caused you to pass, don't make the same mistake again.

◆

Keep in mind that officiating is temporary and your family is permanent.

◆

If officials will work hard to succeed at each of the 150 plays, one play at a time, they will be rewarded with a great game and a long career.

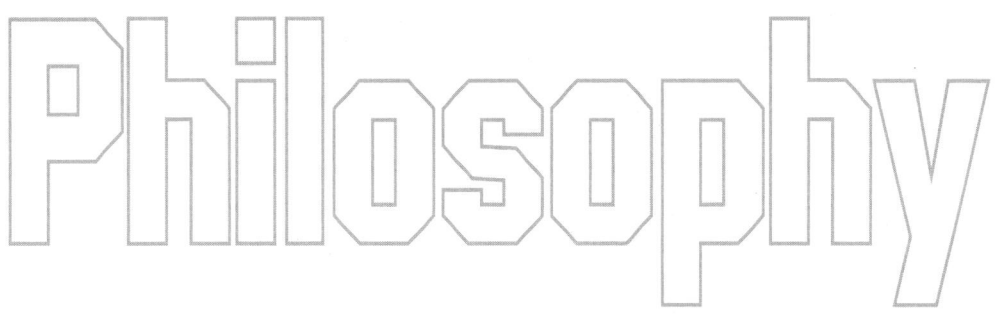

Philosophy

The NFL has provided some of the best opportunities for some of the worst influences on aspiring officials.

◆

Everybody knows better and has the right answer on Monday.

◆

Never practice officiating. Game-like conditions and thought about each play prepare for not needing to "get up" after the opening kick-off.

◆

Officiating is an "eye" not an "ear" kind of job.

◆

If you pay officials peanuts, you get monkeys trying to run the zoo on the field.

◆

A homogenized officiating conference keeps the cream from rising to the top.

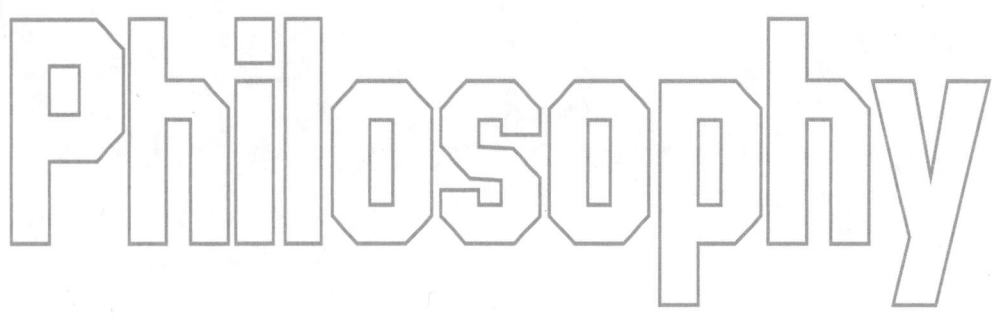

Philosophy

When you start thinking that in a week or two you will be feeling "as good as ever," you are into the final "quarter" of your career.

◆

A retentive memory may be a good thing, but the ability to forget is a true gift. Retain football rules and forget arguments with coaches.

◆

There are many more badly coached and played games than badly officiated games.

◆

There are times when you choose between being human and following the rule book… The best officials know the difference.

◆

A nice goal is to try to erase the thin line between a good game and a great game.

◆

In officiating, contentment is simply refined indolence.

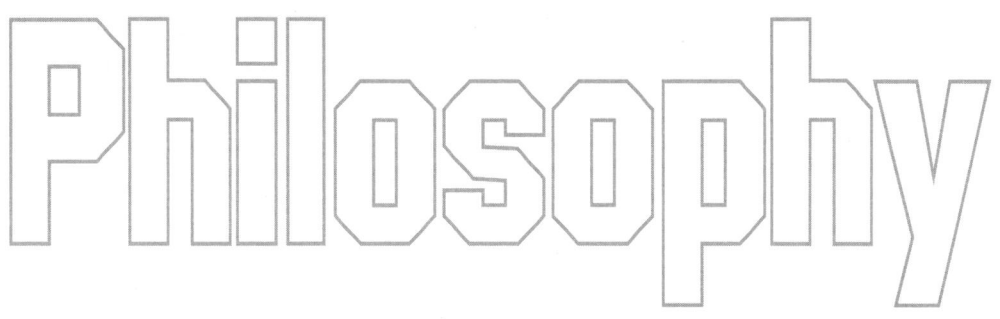

Philosophy

Nothing is more difficult in your career than to drop from your memory an officiating mistake that you are trying to forget.

❖

One of the most difficult things in officiating, and also a great compliment, is to officiate a great game with a lot of opportunities for it to go south and have no one notice who officiated the game.

❖

There is nothing wrong with making mistakes in officiating; it is part of the game. Just do as all those who win on the field do, and do so in moderation.

❖

Are you a young official of promise or simply one of the promises? (Permanent Potential)

❖

Your judgment on the football field, as a successful official is simply the opinion that you have survived.

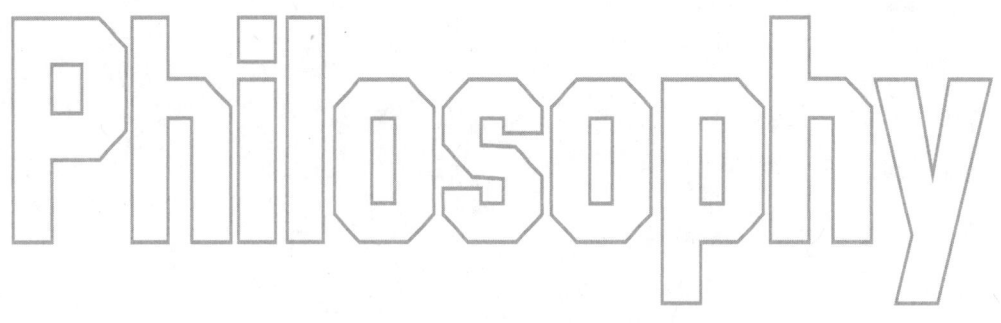

Philosophy

Be patient if you are determined and strong, your time and opportunity will find you.

———◆———

Illusion is the first part of approaching confusion.

———◆———

Average officials imitate good officials…Good officials steal ideas from the best.

———◆———

Talent + persistence = Good officiating.

———◆———

The fastest way to get relief from a game that has gotten out of control is to simply find ways to "slow it down."

———◆———

What you get "free' in officiating, cost much more later in your career.

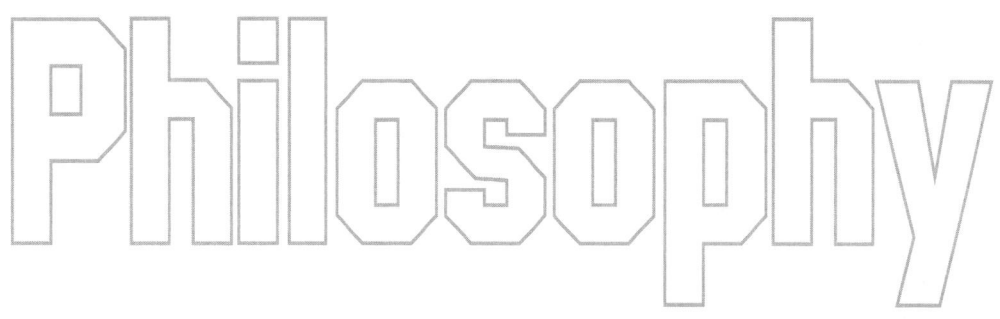

Philosophy

Remember not having the opportunity to work the "big game" of the season is sometimes a wonderful stroke of luck.

◆

Sometimes "dull" games can still be entertaining. Work the game and have fun.

◆

The time to relax during a difficult and stressful game to officiate is when you believe you don't have time to do it.

◆

Coaches and officials all have one thing in common — They are all different.

◆

Officiating talent is cheaper than rock salt. Hard work is what separates the field.

◆

It is possible to be so careful trying to correctly officiate a "big game" that you can stumble over even the simple things.

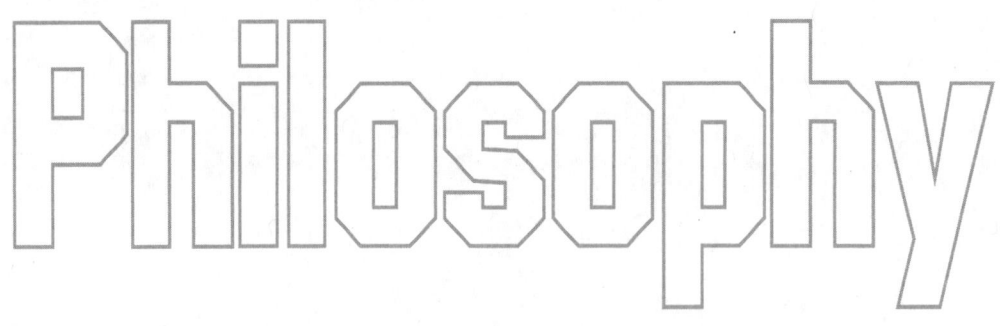

Philosophy

"Playing it safe" as an official also has its dangerous side.

―◆―

Officiating is easy when you don't know how, but very difficult when you do.

―◆―

If you don't "risk" as an official, you "risk" even more.

―◆―

Officiating is too important to take too seriously. Be professional, good and have fun.

―◆―

It seems weird, but if you are kind to officials and coaches who don't respect themselves, they will also have no respect for you. Continue to be professional, just be aware.

―◆―

Some officials and coaches under pressure carry moderation into excess.

Philosophy

The chief object to improving as an official is not to "learn" things, but to "unlearn" things from previous experiences.

◆

The best way out of a tough experience is to work through it and not sweep it under or go around.

◆

For some of us, officiating a very difficult and challenging game is the most natural form of relaxation and satisfaction one can achieve.

◆

When the game has ended and the crowd is rushing on to the field, try to separate together in a bunch.

◆

The best way to manage some mistakes is to take advantage of the next "break" that occurs in the game.

Philosophy

Sometimes you need to use your memory to forget some unpleasant officiating experiences to keep the playing field "level" for players, coaches and officials.

―◆―

Mistakes will be made in each game by each official. If you look back too often during the season, you will soon be headed the wrong direction.

―◆―

If you are going to profit from your mistakes, you are going to make some.

―◆―

Excellent officiating is a habit.

―◆―

When you are about to lose your temper with a player, coach, or another official, remember that anger usually begins with a mistake, followed by a regret.

―◆―

If your goal is to have everyone point out your faults, start giving them a lot of advice.

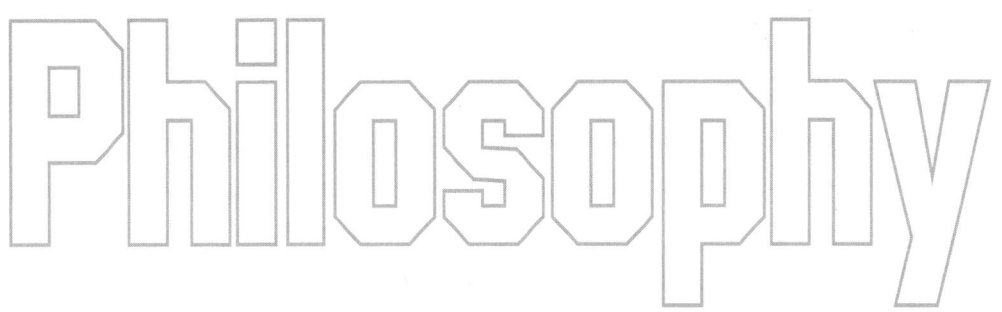

Philosophy

Try to exhibit "maturity" a few years before you retire.

◆

In officiating a difficult football game adversity introduces an official to his position and responsibility on the field.

◆

If you have had a tough game, but missed the meaning of what went wrong, you may also miss having a schedule next year.

◆

An official too old to officiate, is at least ten years older than I am.

◆

A good technique for an official is to know when to let a conflict die.

◆

If you have a complicated problem to solve on the field, try approaching a good solution from a different point or view.

Philosophy

When an official is willing to admit he is wrong, he is right.

♦

The best officials can create a great game when conditions are not favorable. The average official may get the job done when everything falls into place and feels good.

♦

Timing is a big part of choosing your retirement date — Try to make sure you are "envied" and not "pitied."

♦

When the best team in the league is playing the poorest team in the league and you prepare for a great game and even keep in mind overtime, you will not be surprised or unprepared for an upset.

♦

You can measure the strength of an official by determining how he recovers from a series of "little things" going wrong.

Philosophy

In the heat of a tough battle, the quickest way to becoming a great official is to learn from others' mistakes, before making the same mistake yourself.

——◆——

In the heat of a tough battle, stay level when things move up or down.

——◆——

Some crews with a few successful games are even more distasteful than their many failures.

——◆——

Some games require that you swim through the crap. The secret is not to "bob" in it.

——◆——

He, who timely hesitates, is usually right.

——◆——

Is your goal to "get there" or to improve and to achieve after you are "there"?

Philosophy

If you have to work hard to be average, be the very best average.

◆

Be careful of the official who is looking for an opportunity to see a situation that he would like to have happen in a game because it can sometimes become a self-fulfilling prophecy.

◆

Take the "tone" of the game you are officiating and make it better.

◆

It is not a compliment to do something very well, if it was done poorly, very well.

◆

Every snap has the possibility of the dawn of a new error.

◆

Big games and big names become larger as the years pass for retired officials.

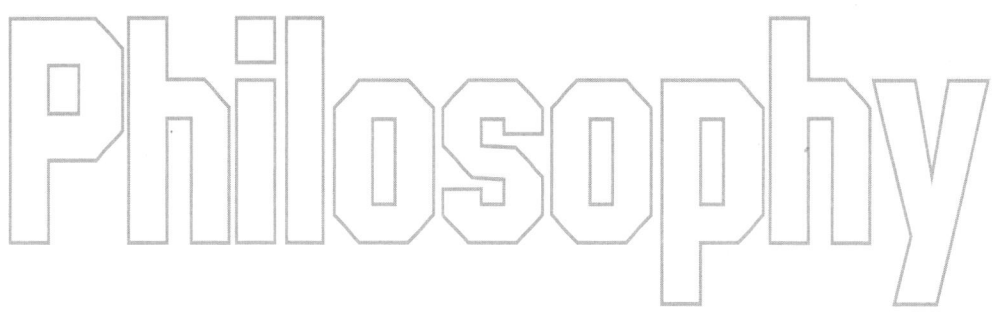

Philosophy

Your career is too short to make enough mistakes to be a successful official. You must learn and improve from the mistakes of others.

───◆───

The best part of a mistake is to learn from it.

───◆───

Experience will make a positive difference if you understand the meaning of that experience.

───◆───

It is a fact that mistakes are made in officiating sports. It is how we recover from errors that counts.

───◆───

If applying the rules of the game doesn't hurt a team, the rules aren't working. Your job is to heal the hurt and produce a healthy game.

───◆───

Every game is truly like a deck of cards; the key is to individually and collectively as a crew, take the hand that you are dealt and try to win.

Philosophy

What shortens officiating careers is the unfortunate circumstances of the poor timing of events and poor choices.

◆

Security in major college officiating doesn't come by "getting there", it is by getting better each game and each season.

◆

A tough, hard-fought, well-played game is a marathon and not a sprint. Keep a pace and flow throughout the game, and it will be fairly decided between the teams.

◆

It is okay to look ahead during the game, just don't look farther ahead than you can see.

◆

Criticism is much easier and sooner forgotten than an insult.

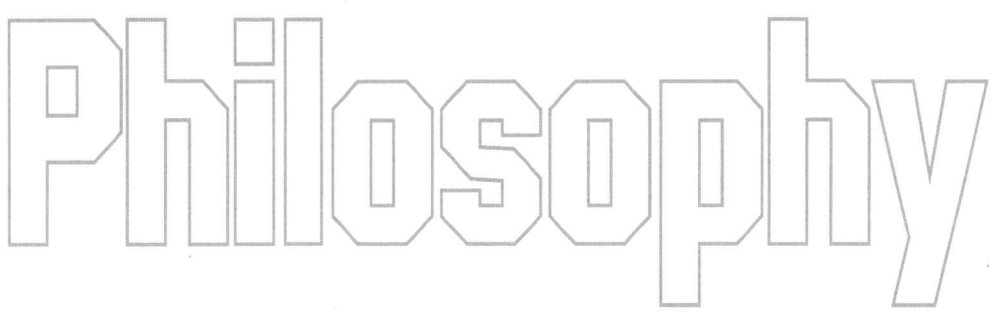

Philosophy

Officiating maturity is the sum total of previous experience used to reduce future mistakes.

◆

Little things cause big things. If you get big plays right, it is because you have given attention to the little things.

◆

If your only goal in officiating is success, you have limited yourself from many other attributes that are much more lasting.

◆

What goes around, comes around. Be flexible as in any given game you can become: the steam roller or the road; the bug or windshield, or the statue or the pigeon!

◆

Situations that feel like a slippery slope or bananas on ice need the grip of common sense.

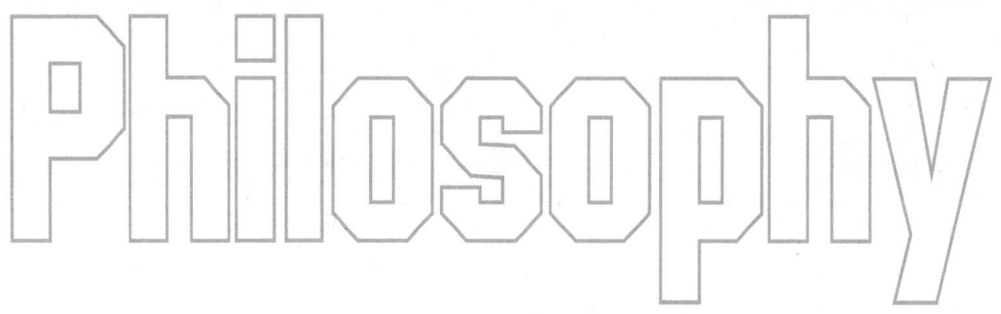

Philosophy

As you near the end of your career be careful, but expect to be blamed for mistakes you didn't make.

◆

Sometimes it is possible to look great, even brilliant and still not be right. Bottom line: It is not important that you look good on a play. It is important that the play is correctly officiated.

◆

Officials improve with experience, but it is the capacity of dealing with experiences and improving that makes the biggest difference in officials.

◆

The quality of common sense in an official is the capacity to see things as they are, and then do what needs to be done.

◆

If you have been officiating for 25 years or longer, the vulnerability factor slips into the equation — In that you are accused of things you never did or praised for things that never happened.

Philosophy

It is much better to know that you deserved a Bowl Game and not get one, than to have one and not deserve it. Or an even worse case, have those who know football ask why.

---◆---

Officials should not be judged by their qualifications, but how they make use of their qualities on the field.

---◆---

Officials are divided into two classes: Those who want to become someone, and those who want to accomplish something.

---◆---

You can determine the quality of an official by the mistakes he makes.

---◆---

There are many compromises and "no calls" in a football game. The key is to never sacrifice a rule or principle of the game when officiating.

Philosophy

You do what you are as an official, then you simply become what you do.

───◆───

Fourth and goal, score tied — Wishbone or backbone?

───◆───

The fear of doing what is right at a critical time in the game is grand treason when tension is high and everything is on the line.

───◆───

Sometimes, during a very difficult situation, the only real choice we have as an official is to remain in charge of our attitude about the situation.

───◆───

Once the game is over, all of the players, coaches, and officials go back in the same box. There is life after football.

───◆───

The difference between an official with courage and a coward is the ability to throw the flag or blow the whistle when it is the right thing to do.

Philosophy

Your temper can get you in trouble — Just don't let your pride keep you there until it is too late.

◆

A game has a positive flow when it is perceived to have a natural consequence of consistency while applying the basic philosophy of the rules of the game of football.

◆

The road to a successful football game has several tempting "parking spaces" along the way. Keep the game moving and avoid parking spaces and detours.

◆

It takes a good official to know when he is defending a football rule, or simply defending a prejudice thought or mistake when visiting with a coach. The higher road is to deliver the right rule interpretation and ethical decision.

Philosophy

The best way to build officiating momentum in a football game is to build small successes one snap at a time.

——◆——

Wearing a bowl ring to the locker room does not imply that you are going to have a great game. It is not credentials, but steady improvement and accomplishments that separates officials from getting to the top and staying on top.

——◆——

Sometime officials are lucky enough to get credit for a successful decision that was forced upon them when no other option was available.

——◆——

It is much easier to be critical after the game than correct on the field during the play.

——◆——

A poor official finds it impossible to recover from a temporary set-back. A good official asks "Why did it happen"?

Philosophy

The perception of consistency is more important than the reality of consistency in officiating a football game.

◆

When you are in a tough situation and it simply can't be improved, don't waste too much energy being dissatisfied or you will miss the next opportunity to get something right.

◆

Rookie officials can do their best to create experience, but the bottom line is that you must undergo it.

◆

The act of having each game worked just a little better than the previous one is simply a journey not a destination.

◆

All games give you opportunities to do things that are not necessary and can get you in trouble. If you don't want to slip, don't go in slippery places.

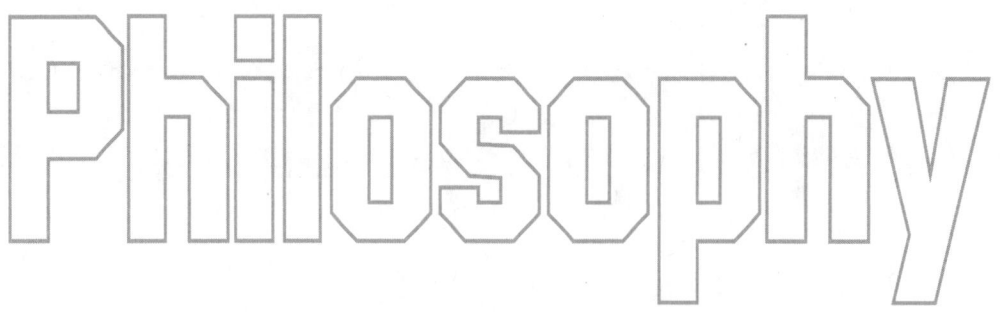

Philosophy

Having a good game and not preparing comes from good luck, not good officiating.

◆

Lots of officials can make the tough call and throw their flag, when the other official sees it first.

◆

Officiating situations that are misapplied and even result in game-changing mistakes can break an official. Officials must remember that this is also an opportunity to become stronger in broken places.

◆

Try to end your career at a ripe old age with the excitement and enthusiasm of your first game.

◆

Seven days of feeling sorry for yourself after making an officiating mistake makes one weak.

◆

If you don't prepare to expect the unexpected, you won't find it.

Philosophy

There is no such thing as "an almost qualified" college official — There is only qualified.

◆

An official's actions on the field are the best interpretation of their thoughts about how they view and understand the game.

◆

In officiating, sometimes the decision is very easy to make because there are no options.

◆

To deserve to rise to the top for a lasting career in officiating, the path is a winding staircase — Using "buddies," "favors," and "relatives" is usually straight up with no pause or hand rails.

◆

You forget most of what others teach you about officiating, but you retain the most through experience. Get a lot of "snaps" to understand the game of football.

Know the difference between urgent and important situations that occur during a football game.

◆

All of us can learn from poor officiating and poor coaching.

◆

Fame in officiating can "come and go," but honesty if lost, cannot return.

◆

All great games are unique and yet very similar to other very special games.

◆

Success is the progressive realization of the worthy goal of improving each game you officiate.

◆

Officiating is more like wrestling than dancing. There is no "routine" (steps), but there is a "flow" to a well-officiated game.

Philosophy

The formula for working a good game when things are going badly: Treat all problems as if they were trivialities, and never treat a triviality as if it were a problem. (Overreacting during an emotional crisis is usually the larger part of the problem.)

◆

It takes a lot of patience as an official to learn to have patience.

◆

It is not the difficult situation in a football game that gets you in trouble, but your reaction to it that determines how you come out of it.

◆

There is not a single play that is so simple that it cannot be officiated wrong in a football game.

◆

Officiating is really: Developing your closest friendships, a special feeling of excitement, some great memories for reflection, and a sense of satisfaction.

Philosophy

The alphabet of a successful officiating career begin with: ability, breaks and courage.

◆

Excellence in officiating does not consist of counting the number of bowl games you have officiated, but whether you deserved working them.

◆

Remember that officiating is a way of travel through life, not a destination.

◆

The key to consistent success in officiating is to develop the patience to do the simple routine situations in a game perfectly, which will give you the skill to do the difficult things easily.

◆

There is no greater quality needed to become a great official than one's desire.

◆

You have not done your job as an official if you got it almost right.

Philosophy

Those officials most preoccupied with their "bowl" assignments are usually the least deserving.

◆

If you have a choice to get to the top, use the ladder and not the elevator.

◆

The test of any official is what he does after the first kick-off.

◆

Winners don't whine, they dedicate their skills to winning.

◆

It is not difficult to be a good official every other week. The key is to be your best every week.

◆

The best officials know that they can be better. Others simply say, "I am not as bad as a lot of officials."

Philosophy

Officials who have a tendency to get "at odds" with a coach, usually fall into the trap of trying to "get even" with a coach.

◆

Officiating "perfection" is an unreachable goal, but its pursuit brings excellence.

◆

Your enthusiasm to officiate a great game is the greatest factor between mediocrity and accomplishment.

◆

Officiate every game as if it could be your last, and your rewards will be greater and your memories even better.

◆

There are many parts to becoming a good official, but it takes no ability to hustle.

Philosophy

Everything will come to good officials if they wait, as long as they are improving while they are waiting.

———◆———

The difference between an "improving" official and one getting "worse," is how he responds to a mistake.

———◆———

It is how you deal with failure on the football field one week that determines how you achieve success the following week.

———◆———

The only real mistake in officiating is when one learns nothing new to improve on the next game.

———◆———

Knowledge and understanding of officiating advances by steps and not by leaps.

———◆———

If the game you worked last week still seems "big," you are not focused on today's game.

Philosophy

When you make a mistake in a game, you don't lose unless you lose the lesson.

♦

If you want to enjoy major-college officiating, you must earn it first.

♦

In the heat of making a difficult decision, don't major on the details, but focus on the big picture and then work backward to cover your bases.

♦

Remember no matter how great your accomplishments, lots of coaches and officials have helped you to get there.

♦

When an official makes a mistake, whether it be because of "action" or "inaction," he must be held accountable, either way.

Philosophy

The comfort of an "easy" game to officiate does not create the best measure of an official. It is best observed and evaluated when there is strong challenge and controversy.

———◆———

You get the opportunity because of talent. You stay there because of hard work and improvement.

———◆———

You'll never realize how long a week can be until you have had a big mistake in your last game.

———◆———

It is a bad game plan to always expect good luck.

———◆———

You can have one game and look very good for seven days, but football officiating is a series of games over eleven weeks. Try to improve each week and remember that you are no better than your last game.

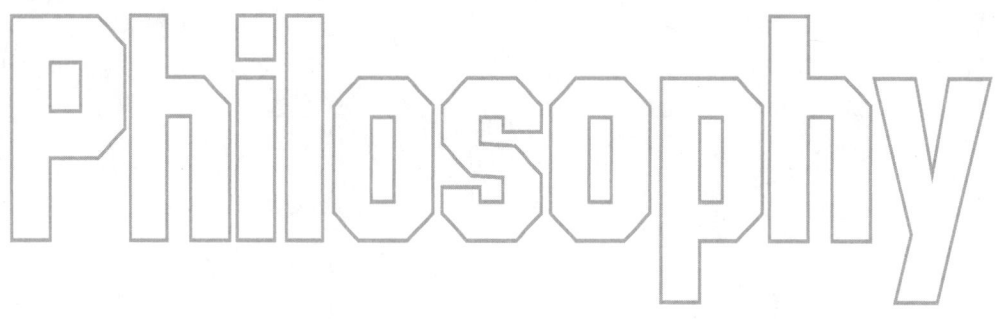

Philosophy

Is it your purpose to officiate a great game, or do you hope to officiate a great game? The difference is significant and self-fulfilling.

◆

Fear is a result of not being comfortable with the unknown. The officials who solve this issue the earliest are the most successful.

◆

Decision vs. indecision? Sharp and clean vs. dull and ragged.

◆

Be careful of determining what your goal is in officiating. Are you trying to make something "for" yourself, or "of" yourself?

◆

There are well-officiated games and poorly officiated games. The bottom line is that you can't keep a good official "down" or a bad official "up."

Philosophy

One good indicator of your officiating success is what you had to give up to get to where you want to be.

◆

Successful officiating is a habit. Unfortunately, so is poor officiating.

◆

When the newspaper and coaches criticize you for a mistake, you have a choice to have it make you bitter or better.

◆

Your legacy in officiating should be bigger than leaving some memories and a reputation…Leave a footprint for others.

◆

Nothing matters less than how you officiated last week.

◆

"Game-like" conditions are the best practice if you are focused on improving.

Philosophy

When an official recognizes a fault, it is half corrected.

At the college level of officiating, ability is similar. It is the official's will to improve that separates everyone.

It is much better to solve or prevent problems early than to wait until the second half and deal with a crisis or two.

To rise in the ranks of officiating, you must be on the level.

Some officials have two reasons for their mistakes. 1). A good one. 2). The real one.

Don't pretend to be the official you don't intend to be.

Philosophy

You cannot become a great official by comparing yourself with good officials.

♦

One bitter lesson learned is better than ten "atta boys."

♦

An official with too many irons in the fire can't help but have a few cool off.

♦

The only good luck you need to a officiate a great football game is the ability to overcome bad luck.

♦

A well-officiated game today will not be based on previously well-officiated games or bad games, but on your preparation for this game.

♦

When you make a decision that is "half right," it is also "half wrong."

Philosophy

Officials, who try to whittle others down are little people trying to reduce you to their size.

———◆———

A football game is a series of battles; teams win some and lose some, and officials make correct and incorrect calls. The goal is to have the game won by the team who deserves to win.

———◆———

When officials see the "handwriting on the wall" and all they can do is criticize the formation of the letters, the spelling and meaning are cast in stone.

———◆———

Two things can be bad for an official's heart, running in circles and running other crew members down.

———◆———

All officials live in one of two tents, content or discontent.

———◆———

Anger manages everything badly, including common sense.

Philosophy

The wind of anger blows out the lamp of common sense when things are tense on the field.

◆

Don't spoil the game you are working by wishing for another game. Your loss of concentration will ruin one game and keep you from working the one you wish to work.

◆

It is okay to wish and hope for "good luck," just don't depend on it.

◆

When no one on the crew measures up to you, check your yardstick.

◆

Whether you are a "has been" or a "will be" is determined by attitude, not by age or experience.

◆

If you don't have the courage to correct a mistake made by someone else on the field, you are not entitled to criticize the play after the game.

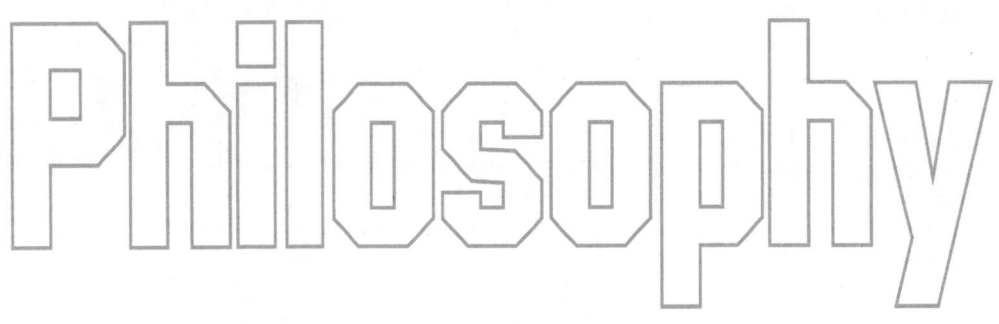

Philosophy

Mistakes are easier to deal with earlier in your career. Get them out of the way, survive and then increase the interval of time between them.

——◆——

The cure for a "sick game" is to create a flow followed by a ritual of positive routines.

——◆——

When officials base their decisions on what is fair and appropriate, 95% of their interpretations of the rules of the game have already been made.

——◆——

The dilemma: Patience taken to an extreme is perceived as courage.

——◆——

Be prepared: Nothing that goes wrong ever happens at the right time.

——◆——

Sometimes the secret of working a great game depends on what you don't do.

Philosophy

A true enemy in your officials' association is better than a false friend.

◆

The best vitamin for improving a crews' morale is B-one.

◆

The best way to get even with a coach or player, who has embarrassed you, is to forget it.

◆

A poorly officiated game doesn't mean that you are a poor official; it is just going to take a little longer to succeed.

◆

Having a good plan and getting a good night's sleep, is much better than lying awake the night after a game not sleeping because of what you didn't do.

◆

"Bumps" in a game mean that you are either headed for a rut or coming out —This is your choice.

Philosophy

The more preoccupied an official is with his bowl games, the usually the less deserving he is of the games.

——◆——

Just because you skipped by, doesn't mean you are polished.

——◆——

Don't overestimate the decency of a guy wanting to take your place on the field as an official.

——◆——

When the crew is mediocre, the best official on the crew is at risk!

——◆——

Improvement in officiating is using experiences to reduce and eventually, eliminate all guessing related to decisions made on the field.

——◆——

The key to surviving an embarrassing, awkward time in the game is to simply keep going.

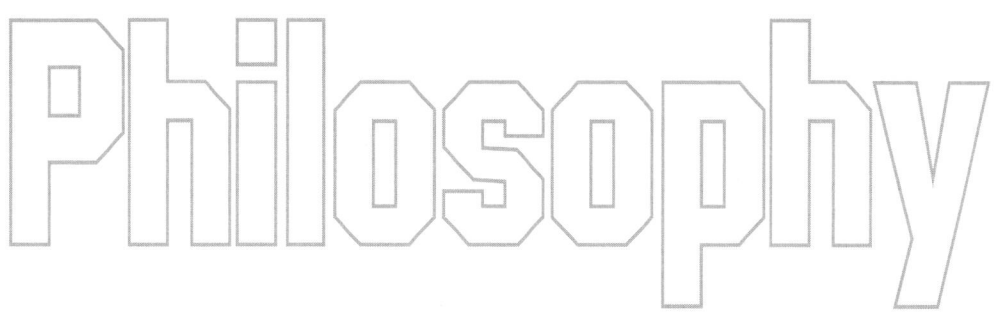

Philosophy

The secret to a well-officiated game is continuous success with the small things that occur during the game

———◆———

The path to officiating a great game always has a few puddles; just avoid the elephant traps.

———◆———

It is easy to know what you would do in a difficult situation if you know that you will never have that opportunity.

———◆———

If you make a game "difficult to work," you should not get credit for working a "difficult" game.

———◆———

Those officials on their way up need to be respectful of those on their way down.

———◆———

A coach or official who professes to "know all of the rules" — Provides a lot of suspicion.

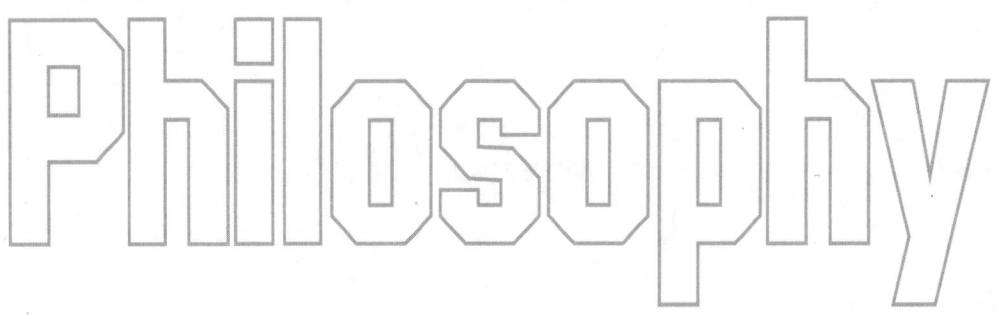

Philosophy

The mistakes an official makes in a game are much more forgivable than those he tries to hide.

◆

If one official simply has a "gut feeling" he is right and the other six have no information but support his decision, there is a greater chance he is wrong than right.

◆

Don't be a part of a crew with the greatest opportunities and worst influence on your philosophy of officiating.

◆

There has been an abuse of statistics and a lack of common sense for anyone who brags of officiating the "perfect game."

◆

If the average official makes more mistakes than you do, how good are you?

Section 10

"Poor Officials"

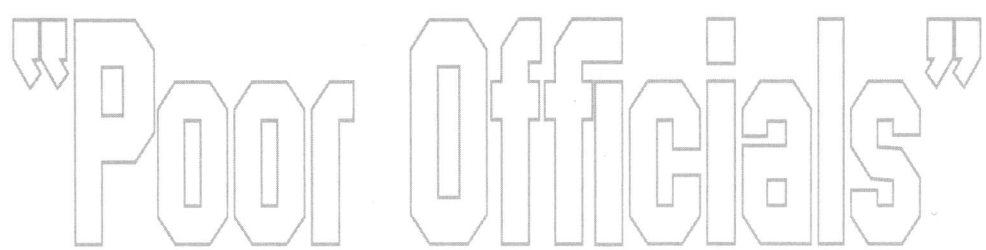

"Poor Officials"

This section is everything you wanted to know about poor officiating, but were afraid to ask OR possibly not comfortable saying to an official in person. Those fans who simply don't like sports officials may read this section first! If this is your choice, I suggest you read the chapters on Coaches and Humor next, in order to try to balance either your anger or sense of humor. Sports officials may also move quickly to this section, especially if their self-esteem needs to be tested. Seriously, this is a good review of things that officials need to avoid if they want to improve.

An official who "makes up" a call to "even things up," simply creates the ill feeling of hope over experience.

———◆———

Officials who fail, fall into two categories: Those who thought about it and never followed through; and those who officiated, but never gave any thought to the game.

———◆———

The perfect example of an official trying to "get to the top" who has no ability: He simply manages to make no decision on the field and escapes all responsibility for what happens.

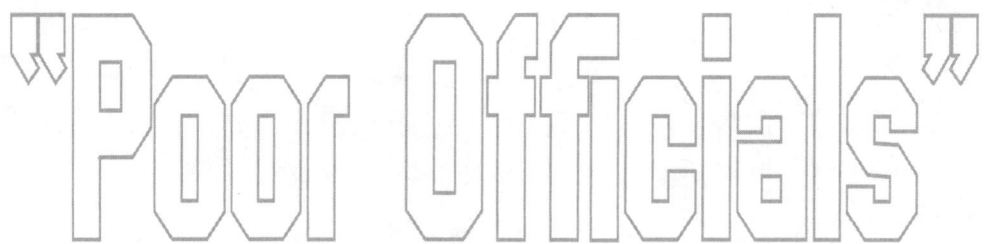

The worst disease an official can have is nervous ability.

◆

An easy way to become a poor official is to pretend that you are good.

◆

Rudeness is a poor official's weak imitation of strength.

◆

The hardest job in officiating is trying to look good when you are not.

◆

Making exceptions to the rules of football or rationalizing integrity, is the quick decline of each individual as well as the crew.

◆

The longer you dwell on your mistakes, the greater their power to distract and cause a problem for you.

◆

10% of the officials make 90% of the mistakes, and also have 90% of the excuses.

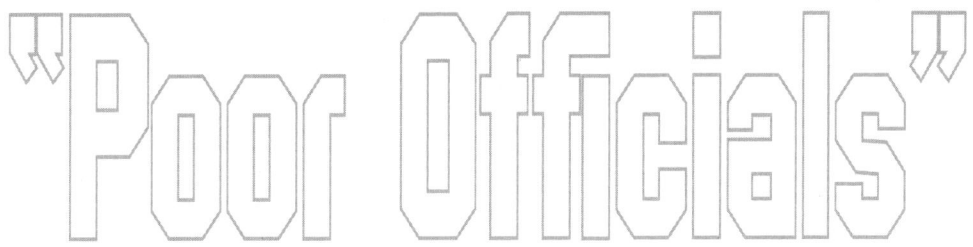

"Poor Officials"

Verbal shots about officials who work your position are really a sign of simple jealousy without a halo.

◆

It is not a compliment to be called an "experienced" official. "Experience" is the term everyone uses for their mistakes.

◆

The greatest mistake an official can make is being afraid. The second greatest mistake is throwing the flag when you are afraid.

◆

If it is the goal of an official to become a major-college official and not improve after "arriving," the spinning door will kick you in the butt on your way out.

◆

Have you ever noticed that the faults for which officials tend to criticize others for, are often the ones we see in them?

"Poor Officials"

The short memory of a poorly officiated game is the conscience of an official who will never improve.

◆

Pessimistic officials are not effective, but they do have a couple of advantages. They are either constantly being proven that they are right all along or simply pleasantly surprised.

◆

Officials who cannot motivate themselves will never be better than "average," regardless of their talents.

◆

Weak officials will only survive in fair weather (easy games). When it starts to rain (the game becomes tough), they drown in every drop.

◆

No official is really lost at his position. He is easily found, but just don't belong.

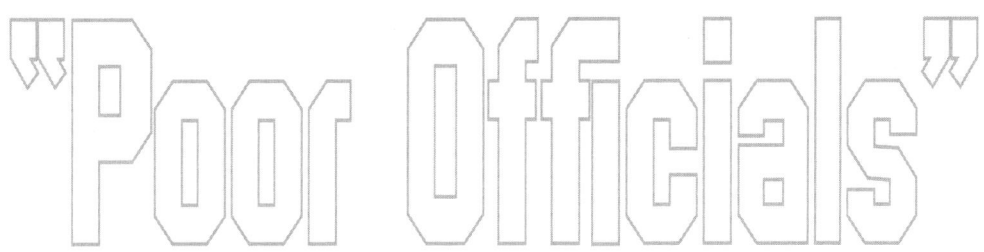

"Poor Officials"

Getting even, making up a call, showing a player or a coach up, is the last refuge of an incompetent official.

◆

An official who is not truthful has two problems: First, he is not believed. Second, he will not believe others.

◆

Great officials have their limitations; but stupid officials have no boundaries.

◆

Officials who simply disguise themselves as "good officials" eventually fool themselves by creating a disguise that even they can't detect.

◆

Some officials flash brilliance nearly to the top of their striped socks.

◆

The confidence of an ignorant official will always be overcome by his indecision of knowledge.

"Poor Officials"

Mediocre officials recognize their level and work hard to stay there. Those with talent work to improve.

Some officials will never learn anything for this reason — They understand everything too soon.

The only thing nice about being the poorest field judge in the conference is that it brings joy to the next official to take your place.

A blind official: 20/20 sight and no vision of the game.

The official who always excuses himself, accuses himself.

Foolish consistency is the wrongful joy in the minds of little minds.

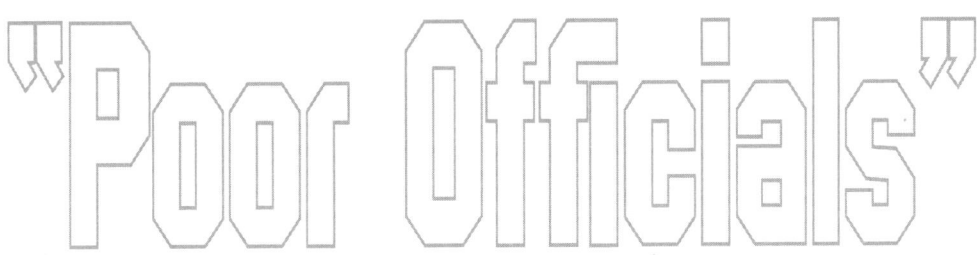

"Poor Officials"

Keeping score of old scores and scars, getting even and one-upping, always make you less of an official.

◆

Some "good ole' boy" officials associations are organized to effectively allow their buddies to reach their highest level of incompetence.

◆

A mediocre football official is always at his best.

◆

Some officials immature with experience.

◆

Is a sloppy uniform, poor pregame and officiated game caused by ignorance or apathy? And of course, the response from the mediocre official is, "I don't know and I don't care."

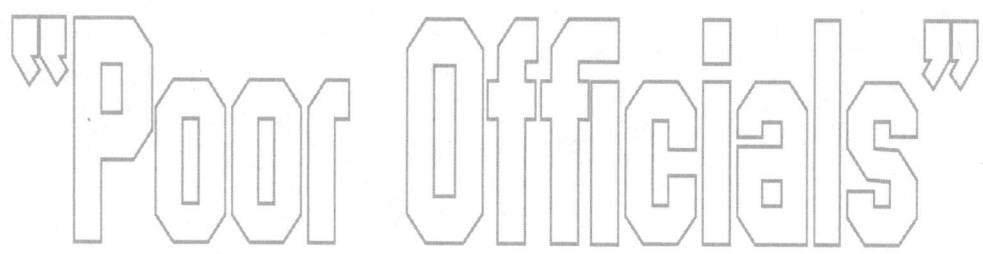

"Poor Officials"

If you are not making any mistakes, you have two issues: 1). You don't understand the game. 2). You are not trying hard enough to apply the rules of the game.

◆

Some officials who don't improve stumble over getting the play right, and then hurry along as if nothing has happened.

◆

Over-officiating is under-whelming.

◆

He is a self-made official who owes his lack of success to no one.

◆

See the play, make the call…Be a "ready, aim, fire official," not "ready, aim, aim, aim…" Don't be known as "His indecision was final."

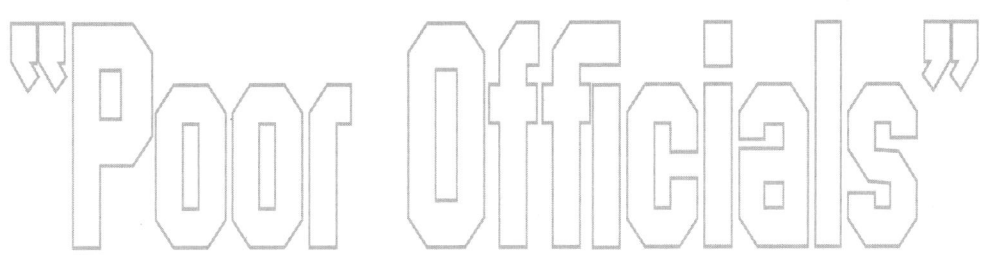

"Poor Officials"

I always question the official who tells me he is "burned out," because I wonder if he was ever on fire.

◆

Mediocre officials never improve because their best recollection of their mistakes is a bad memory.

◆

Some officials, when they hit rock bottom after a bad call, continue to dig.

◆

There are two kinds of officials who never amount to much: Those who cannot do what they are told, and those who can simply do nothing else but what they are told.

◆

Some officials are so critical, their prejudice become plausible to other weak officials.

"Poor Officials"

Labels to avoid: "Woulda/coulda," "Permanent potential," "Many talents, all minor," and "A professional amateur."

◆

If you don't know what a well-officiated game feels like, you will never touch one.

◆

There are lots of ways to become a failure in officiating, but indecision is the most successful.

◆

Show me a thoroughly satisfied official and I will show you one on his way down.

◆

Officials can be a very jealous breed. Keep in mind that their envy is the sincerest form of flattery.

◆

Nothing is more terrible or looks worse on the field than ignorance in action.

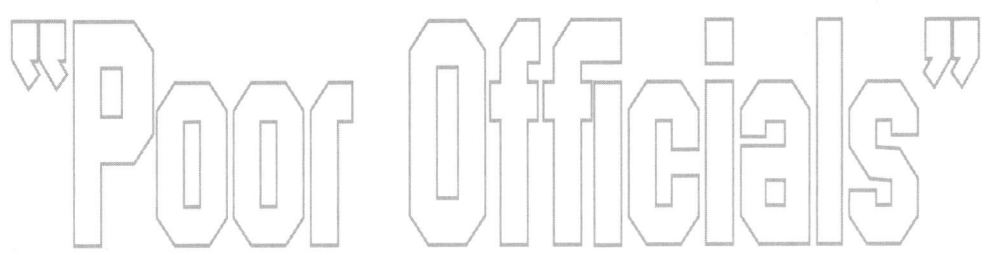

Poor officials are more interested in placing the blame, than getting the play correct.

♦

The easiest way to grow small when officiating is trying to be greater than the game.

♦

It is difficult to improve when your only critic is the mirror.

♦

Enthusiasm: Good officials have it; poor ones never will.

♦

Poor officials are made not born.

♦

The classic worst-case poor official: An inferior person with a superiority complex.

♦

Being a failure-conscious official always has a self-fulfilling ending.

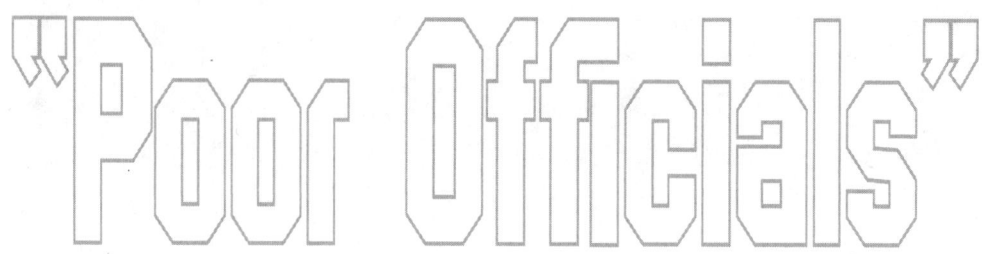

An official with no confidence can hardly wait for the game to end so he can look back on it with regret.

◆

Whiners are the products of a sour grapes philosophy.

◆

Officials who are promoted for the wrong reasons often complain about the quality of others.

◆

Poor officials are similar to cars: When they start knocking they are having internal problems.

◆

Vanity is the quicksand for making common sense decisions.

◆

If an official continues to tell you he is "not a bad official," the crew will soon become suspicious of him.

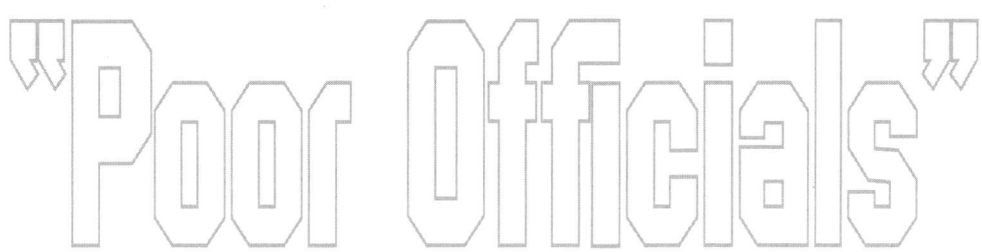

"Poor Officials"

When regrets take the place of dreams, officials are on their way down.

◆

Poor officials stay busy with things that do not matter on the field.

◆

The real advantage of being a book official is that they can organize their ignorance and hide their common sense.

◆

Ignorance of the rules is a problem, but a bigger one is thinking we know the rules when we don't.

◆

Doing little, often, is a consistent habit of a poor official.

◆

Experienced, below-average officials recognize a mistake right after they repeat it.

"Poor Officials"

Ignorance can sometimes simply be innocence. For bad officials, stupidity comes with experience.

♦

Preparation will find a way. Indifference will find an excuse.

♦

If an official does not have what it takes to be a "good" official, and he asked for advice — Don't put a carrot at the end of the hole he is digging — Be honest.

♦

Crews who bring manure to the game attract new flies and a crappy game.

♦

When a poor official makes a mistake, he is the second to admit it.

♦

Poor officials have an almost infinite capacity for taking things for granted.

Section 11

Pregame

THE PREGAME: (L/R: Paul Brown, John Laurie and Len Williams). It was always my approach to a pregame to have a football field with "offense/defense" symbols, in order to simulate situations that might occur during the game.

Pregame is a time set aside for the referee (crew leader) to meet with the crew before the game to discuss situations that may occur in the contest. It allows them an opportunity to discuss how they are going to be handling a variety of plays that they must handle properly, individually, and as a crew. It is a time when officials prepare mentally and emotionally to officiate their best game. A pregame will range from 30 minutes to two hours, depending on the crew, their interest, and frankly their dedication to officiating. Author's note: Pregames that I have led have been "cussed" and "praised," but I am very proud to be remembered as a referee who had thoroughly planned (sometimes lengthly) discussions in which the entire crew prepared to work their best games individually and collectively.

A good pregame reduces officials' excuses for failure.

◆

The perfect pregame is thought of action in reversal.

◆

A good pregame is not how much you cover, but how much you uncover.

◆

One of the real advantages of a disorderly pregame is that throughout the game you will be making exciting discoveries.

A well-officiated football game should have the flow and gentle progression of the pregame revisited.

◆

A good pregame may cover 20% of the exact things that will occur during a game, but this same pregame will prepare you for 90% of what you need to handle the difficult stuff. The last 10% requires luck or a good bounce.

◆

The pregame is an excellent map to officiate a great game. Unfortunately, after the kick-off, the road is always under construction.

◆

In the pregame, winners discuss what they want to happen during the game; losers discuss what they want to avoid.

◆

Never let last week's game use up too much time in this week's pregame. Mechanics and keys are more important than a lengthy discussion about the previous week's game.

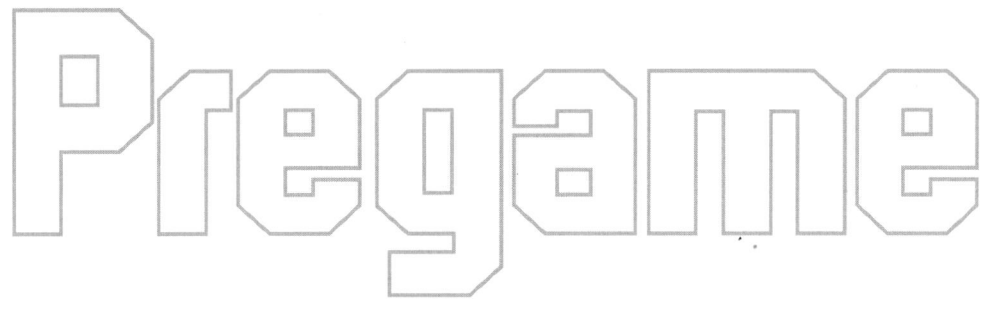

Pregame

Rule book officials can only find problems which the rule book answers. The game is more complicated and has more parts than the simple interpretation of the rule book.

◆

Beware of the "book official" who knows the rules and nothing about the game, but is eager to share it with others on his crew.

◆

During the football pregame, don't be afraid to ask dumb questions; they're easier to handle than dumb mistakes two hours later.

◆

A good pregame is paramount in preparing the crew, but the bottom line is the best worked game is by the crew with the fewest mistakes.

◆

Book officials know the rules; experienced and wise officials know the exceptions.

In some pregames, if you are not confused, you are not paying attention.

◆

A short pregame is the shortest line to disaster.

◆

A split crew pregame can bring friends together and new ideas, but in some cases it can be like salt water; good to swim in but hard to swallow.

◆

Some 60 minute pregames seem as long as a week. While some 60 minute football games (four quarters), unfold like a well-planned pregame.

◆

I truly believe in the value of a good pregame, but "well done" on the field is much better than "well said" at the pregame.

Pregame

The first time you say, "The pregame is stupid," write down the date and time; because the day will come when you want to know the exact moment your officiating career began its decline.

◆

The idea of a brief, incomplete pregame, should not be tossed aside lightly. It should be thrown with great force.

◆

One of the great disadvantages of hurrying through the pregame is that you can spend a long time on the field trying to recover.

◆

In theory there should be no difference between a great pregame and the game itself. But in the game different things happen, and those appropriate adjustments are the difference in a great game and a well-officiated game.

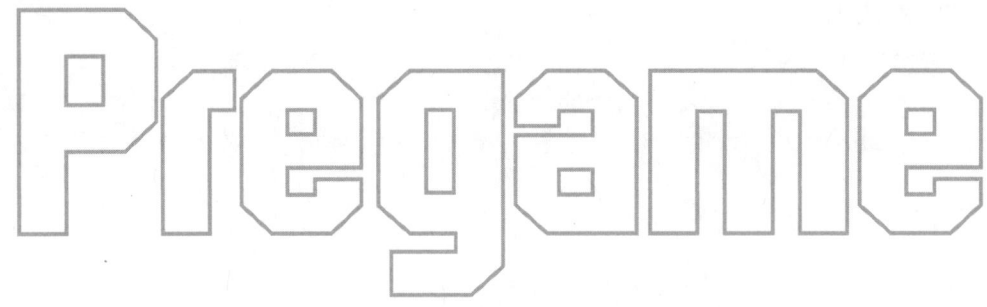

Sometimes discussing the "what if's" that can occur in a game can reveal something that could be important that is obscured without the original discussion. (Don't spend a lot of time trying to understand this one, or frankly on "what if's during the pregame.)

◆

A few loose ends during a pregame can give seven men enough rope to hang themselves during a football game.

◆

In a pregame, you can tell whether an official is clever by his answers; you can also tell if he is wise by his questions.

◆

Every crew has baggage. The more baggage that is "checked" at the pregame, the less chance for excess during the game.

Pregame

Problems at the pregame can be addressed one at a time. They become more complex after the kick off, when they get out of line.

◆

An effective pregame is the shorthand to a well officiated football game.

◆

A referee without a good pregame is like a balloon with a slow leak.

◆

A good pregame goes a long way to eliminate the crews' individual or collective excuse for failure.

◆

If during the pregame or during the game, you expect your crew to read between the lines, it will be helpful if you write big.

◆

A 30-minute pregame is perfection of means and confusion of ends.

Pregame

No single pregame format succeeds after the first kick-off.

◆

A pregame without action is a daydream. Action without a pregame is a nightmare.

◆

The trick for a successful pregame is to have the crew think they are thinking, but you are really asking for trouble and confusion if you really try to make them think.

◆

Ridicule and sarcasm are the deadliest weapons against a great pregame.

◆

If your last game was a disaster, don't spend too much time in next week's pregame on last week's vomit. Review a few "big things" and get on with preparing for a new positive opportunity.

Pregame

The will to officiate a perfect game is not even close to being as important as preparing to work a great game.

◆

To have a pregame that is not meaningful to the game that is going to occur in two hours is like writing an important letter, not addressing it, and tossing it in the mailbox.

◆

Nothing is more certain in a pregame than knowing that uncertainties will occur after the first kick off.

◆

If you are in a pregame rut, the only difference between that and an official's graveyard is depth.

◆

A football game without a pregame is lame, and a pregame that does not include the very basics of the game is blind.

Pregame

It is not the pregame that will "save" you when things get "tough" during the game, it is the good planning and discussion during the pregame that will pull you through.

———◆———

If you are poorly prepared for the game, the first kick-off begins on the far side of despair.

———◆———

A good pregame does not require "big-time" wisdom, but it can prevent "big-time" errors.

———◆———

The concept of planning (pregame) does not ensure situations discussed will occur, but it does ensure that everyone in the crew is prepared.

———◆———

If the purpose of your pregame is to leave nothing to chance, you will do a few things well. However, you will miss some key spontaneous components to officiating a great football game.

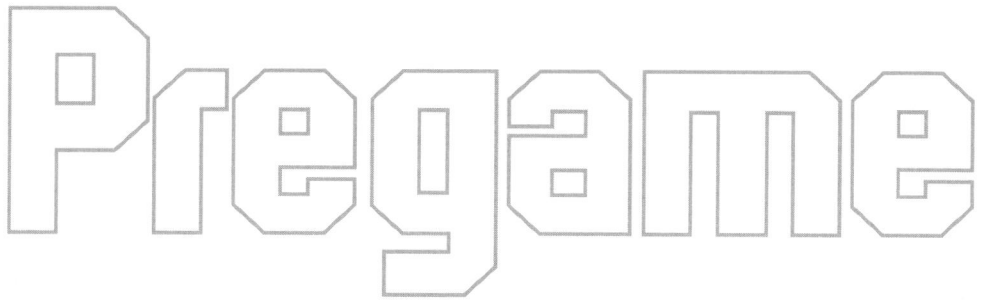

Pregame

Question: Do you "officiate" differently in the pregame than after the kick-off? Either way, you can be better.

◆

The most effective pregame is not designed to predict a play-by-play analysis of what is going to happen on the field, but to clearly conceived goals and expectations.

◆

The pregame determines what needs to happen on the field — Find a way.

◆

If you don't have a plan in your pregame for what you want to happen on the field, you must simply settle for what you are given.

◆

A poor pregame allows officials to dimly see what is ahead in the game versus seeing clearly ahead with an appropriate pregame.

Pregame

A good pregame will prepare and prevent situations that during the game will need repair and repent.

◆

The most important thing about a pregame is to have one.

◆

Percentages favor a well-planned pregame for reaching its intended destination.

◆

For some officials, unfortunately, after a good pregame, brain dialysis starts with the kick-off and ends on the last play of the game.

◆

If you approach your preparation for a good pregame like a pig, I am pretty sure you will come back feeling like sausage.

◆

Pregame

Some crew members during the pregame have really frightened me. I simply hoped at the opening kick-off they had pulled their heads out and their brains moved to their heads.

◆

A poor pregame is similar to being shipwrecked before you even board.

◆

A crew with a poor pregame burns their bridges before they get to them.

◆

Cutting corners in the pregame usually means you are going in a circle by the end of the first quarter.

◆

The road of a poorly planned pregame is always in need off repair.

◆

Officials whose pregame is designed to prepare for an "easy street" game, have only prepared for a "blind alley" situation.

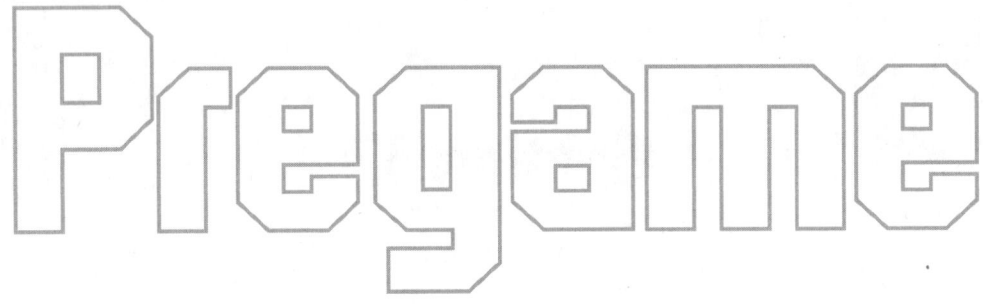

When your pregame plan makes your game strategies unworkable, you are working with a bad pregame.

◆

Constructive experiences and a good pregame are yesterday's answers to potential "game day" problems.

◆

Don't talk "cream" during the pregame conference, and perform like skim milk on the field.

◆

The best pregame prepares you for what is most likely to happen — Not what is most likely not to happen.

Section 12

Referees

the REFEREE and his crew: (L/R) Poncho Girard, Len Williams, Paul Brown, Richard Whittenburg, J.D. Cleavinger and Tim Crowley.

Referees

This is my favorite section because I was a referee in the Big 8 and Big XII Conference for 24 years! The referee is the "crew chief" who is in charge of the officiating crew and "by rule" in charge of the game. As mentioned in section 6 (Leadership), this section is about planning, organizing, and carrying out the functions that need to be addressed in an athletic contest, not unlike the functions of the President or, C.E.O. of an organization. I am confident that you will find many quotations that will carry over into any role you play as a leader in your work or home responsibilities.

The best referee will be able to take a tough situation (multiple fouls, an emotional play or problem, etc.) and have the ability to draw an appropriate conclusion with sometimes inaccurate and insufficient information.

———◆———

The power of any football crew is the ability of the referee to generate effective relationships within the crew.

———◆———

In rare cases, sometimes you must forget the rules and do what is right.

When the referee receives bad information on top of bad information, all that you can ask for is a fair solution to an unfair situation.

◆

It is difficult to lead your crew on to the field if you don't look good wearing a white hat.

◆

Referees who jump to conclusions usually jump over the facts and then misapply a rule.

◆

A good referee isn't concerned about his own career as much as the careers of his crew.

◆

The referee's real danger of becoming a major obstruction to the flow of the game is simply to make an inappropriate decision when enough good information was available to get the call right.

Referees

It is really easy to find referees who are leaders —
They have people wanting to be on their crew.

One of the toughest calls for a referee is to determine the difference between having patience and showing indecision.

The position of "referee" on a crew makes good leaders better and poor leaders worse.

What the referee or supervisor expects, the other officials respect.

A good referee does not tell the crew how to do something, but what needs to be done. The crew will demonstrate the ingenuity to be successful.

Ability is what will get you to the top of your position in the conference if the supervisor has no son at the same position.

Referees

A good referee is the straw that stirs the drink.

◆

Some referees run into problems when they try to put a familiar solution to the wrong problem.

◆

The five R's for the referee: R + R − R = R + R. Rules plus Regulations minus Relationships equals Resentment and Rebellion.

◆

A referee and his crew are invisible when things are going smoothly during the game. The referee steps up and becomes very visible when leadership of a situation is required.

◆

Some of the greatest love affairs I have known involved one referee unassisted.

◆

Referees: Don't smother your crew; no one can grow in the shade.

If your crew is full of willing officials, find out which are willing to work a great game and which are willing to let others.

◆

The best referees find the good in the crew and praise it.

◆

Every referee should have a fair-sized cemetery in which to bury the faults of his crew.

◆

When as a referee you encounter seemingly good advice from two good officials that contradicts each other and you have asked the right questions, ignore both and do what you believe is right.

◆

The position of referee does not confer power, but imposes responsibility.

◆

There is a positive correlation between the effective referee and the caliber of the crew that follows him each Saturday.

Referees

The mark of an effective referee as a crew leader is that he always gives more than he gets.

---◆---

The referee, who has already considered all of the options before listening to the three officials who threw their flags, has more than a hearing problem.

---◆---

A good referee will see some good in every member of his crew, even if he needs to squint from time to time.

---◆---

When the referee is trying to work through a multiple-foul situation, he should do what is right, rather than what is convenient.

---◆---

A referee protects his crew by taking a little responsibility for blame, and less than his share of credit for the work of the crew.

A strong referee is the first one out of the tunnel and down the ramp to the field when the crew is in the "follow the leader" mode.

❖

As a referee, work to develop the confidence of your crew, as opposed to their affection.

❖

It pays to be obvious with your signals, especially if you have a reputation or personality to be subtle.

❖

If you have the ability to carry a football game to the perception of "simplicity in flow," it has a feel of excellence.

❖

The reason that this book can be effective for referees is that quotations are a disguise that allows officials to speak freely.

Referees

The best referees are not heroes; they are hero makers.

———◆———

The absolute toughest situation on the field for your crew to resolve will be much easier if you take a deep breath and look at it as if it is an opportunity.

———◆———

The best referees, when dealing with their crew or a coach, are good listeners.

———◆———

A referee first inspires his crew to have confidence in him, and then he inspires the crew to have confidence in themselves.

———◆———

Bring your crew up to a professional level — Surrounding yourself with dwarves does not make you a giant.

———◆———

When a referee conforms to make his crew and coaches happy all of the time, he becomes ineffective and no one is happy.

Referees

Effective referees make crew members believe in them. The best make the crew believe in themselves.

♦

General notions about a rule interpretation are not as safe as your "gut feeling."

♦

The referee is in a position of authority. This is a predicament for the referee who is not a leader.

♦

Twin killers of a successful end to a well-officiated play are: impatience and not applying correct information.

♦

Why not evaluate your crew on what they do well, not what they don't do? If they don't do enough well, THEY have the problem.

Referees

The toughest enemy to overcome in an emotional crew conference, is when the referee is receiving "bad advice" from the most experienced official in the crew.

◆

The very best referees find ways during the pregame and during the game to eliminate the crews' excuses for making mistakes.

◆

Effective referees have the ability to make his crew members feel comfortable, telling him when they think he is headed the wrong direction.

◆

The referee is the captain of his crew. Just like a ship, he won't be effective if every crew member has a steering wheel.

◆

Before a referee can lead his crew, he must belong.

The best referees adapt their leadership style to fit the multiple situations that occur during the game.

◆

Insecure referees would rather die in consensus than survive out on a very small branch.

◆

It is okay to think through a complicated situation slowly; just don't turn on your mic before your words catch up.

◆

Be careful of a crew member who often tries to create confusion out of simple plays. For the referee, it is best to start with how the play ended and work backward in these situations. (Taking his whistle and flag is not a bad idea.)

◆

Some referees are good natured, friendly and likeable until the opening kick-off.

Some referees are not cocky or arrogant. To them, all you need to do is simply ask anyone who matters.

◆

Some referees have always taken great pride in describing themselves as humble.

◆

The best referees have maximum authority and minimum power.

◆

Understand the play before you look at options, or you will find solutions to the wrong situation.

◆

Some referees are willing to admit that they are not always right; but they will also tell you that they have never been wrong.

◆

Attention referees: A poor crew leaks at the top first.

Referees

The referee needs to be careful when making a "crew" decision because of several opinions given to him being distorted as facts.

―◆―

The price of being a great referee is the ability to assume responsibility.

―◆―

The most important aspect of the relationship between the referee and his crew is that both understand who the leader is.

―◆―

The crude leading the crude: A disrespectful referee leading a crew of wannabes.

―◆―

A good referee will not allow a crew decision to be made on the indifference of the majority.

―◆―

Some referees bring success to a crew wherever they go, and some bring success when they go.

Referees

Some referees don't care how the game is going as long as they are in the driver's seat.

◆

It is possible that some referees are simply born to be great officials, some achieve greatness, and there are the others who just grate.

◆

To get the very best from your crew, give them your very best.

◆

If the referee can't discipline himself, he can't discipline or lead others.

◆

In some difficult and emotional crew conversations, it is important for the referee to know what isn't being said.

◆

The referee's success as a crew leader comes from commitment, not from perceived authority.

Referees

A referee can help his crew more by correcting his own faults than trying to correct "crew faults."

◆

Don't trust a referee to control his crew if he has no self control.

◆

The best referees are impressed by the differences in their fellow officials. Others are conscious of their resemblance to each other.

◆

If the referee is looking for a possible new leader for the crew, good followers are usually not the best choice.

◆

In the post-game conversation with the crew, celebrate what you want to see more of.

◆

An insecure referee makes an insecure crew.

When you have multiple solutions to a situation, go back and refigure what the problem really is. What was the foul, and what are the options to that foul?

◆

A referee does not choose sides within his crew; he has the important and difficult task of bringing them together.

◆

The best referee ends up with the best crew if he treats others as "ends" and never "means."

◆

If you (referee) are too far away from your crew, who moved?

◆

A good referee, like a good shepherd, shears his flock once in awhile, but tries not to skin members of his crew.

Referees

If your referee has a philosophy of "push," you will be in the long run more effective than the one with "pull."

❖

Not often, but sometimes, the referee has to work with a crew in which there is not much choice in rotten apples. It is still his job to make applesauce.

❖

The referee who can't make a decision and treats his crew like a steering committee has the same result as four people trying to park your car.

❖

A referee who makes himself indispensable has a great crew. If he believes he is indispensable, his crew is insecure.

❖

You have won your crew as their referee, when they will share their goals, problems, and their rewards with you.

A referee cannot teach something he doesn't know, as he can't come back from where he has never been.

◆

The only time a referee should set himself above his crew is to carry out his responsibilities.

◆

The "white hat" or the "R" on the back of the referee, does not make him a leader, but it does give him the opportunity to be one.

◆

Referees who follow the path of least assistance are soon on their own.

◆

Too many referees are humble and proud of it.

◆

The referee needs to keep in mind that the less some of your crew know, the more eager they are to talk to you about it.

Referees

A referee must avoid the temptation of making a positive conviction without accurate information.

♦

When an official tries to generalize his explanation to the referee, he is less sure of what he is saying.

♦

The first rule of being a referee is that everything is your fault!

Section 13

"Rule Book" Officials

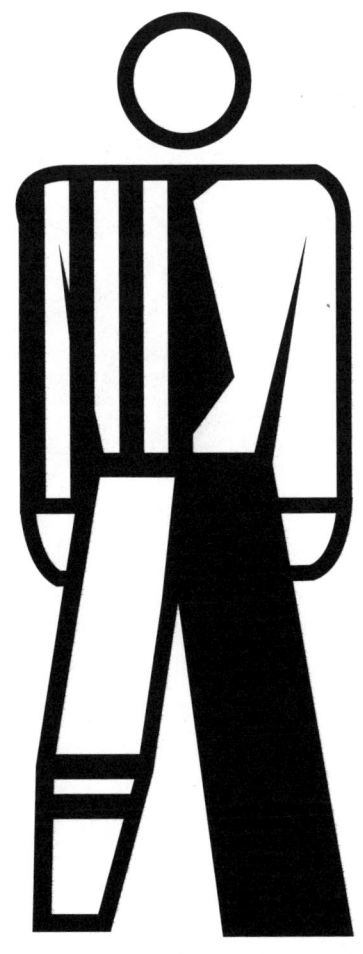

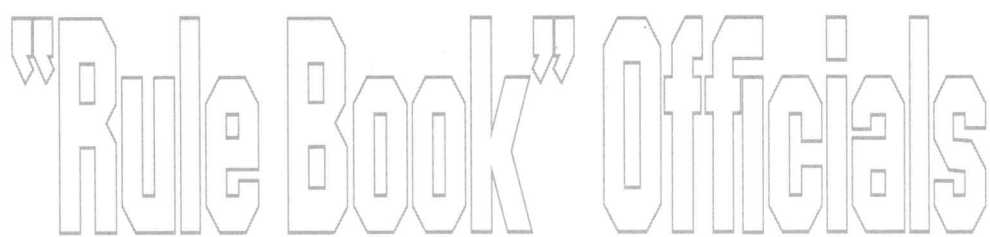

"Rule Book" Officials

This section was fun to put together because it represents an interestesting dichotomy that occurs not only in sports, but also in the business world. Very often in officiating, there are officials who "know the rules" but can't apply what they have learned to the "game." Therefore, the expression "book official." This chapter is sensitive because on the other side is the "official" who believes he understands the "game" — but does not know the rules. Both of these situations are not good for officiating or the sport, but it was fun to take a few "shots" at those who "study" but can't apply what they have learned during the contest.

A football rule book has over 130 pages. The problem begins with the kick off, and after that nothing happens that allows you to follow a script from chapter to chapter, page by page, or even paragraph by paragraph.

◆

His ability to cite rules and explain situations in the pregame leaps across rivers and mountains, but his judgment is only three inches long.

◆

One of the problems of just being a "rule book" official is that you may "die" because of a misprint.

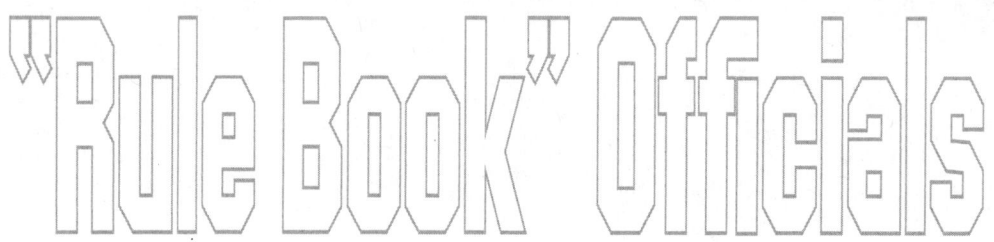

"Rule Book" Officials

A "book" official who can't apply it after the opening kick-off is like the guy who knows 150 ways to make love, but doesn't know any women.

◆

Some officials have the tendency to read PART of the rule book all the way through.

◆

Book officials have a giant brain and a midget's backbone.

◆

If you don't know the rules by now, chances are you are not going to take the time to learn them.

◆

The book official's solution to any problem, is usually as bad as the problem.

◆

Officials are divided into three classes: Those who read and remember, those who read and forget, and those that read and apply every sentence they read on every snap, and never understand the game.

"Rule Book" Officials

The term "common sense" is not found in the rule book index of a "book official."

◆

The rule book is like a fountain, some simply drink and absorb the game, and others continuously gargle.

◆

Some book officials see every plan as a "nail" and their only tool is a hammer.

◆

Officials with integrity and lack of knowledge of rules are simply well intended, poor officials. Book officials without integrity should be removed from officiating.

◆

"One of these days I am going to read the rule book," is really none of these days.

◆

There is a great difference between knowing the rules of football and understanding the game of football.

"Rule Book" Officials

A rule book in the hand is worth two on the shelf.

◆

Once some officials put their rule book down, they simply can't pick it up again.

◆

A book official knows very much about very little and continues to learn more and more about less and less until eventually he knows practically everything about almost nothing at all.

◆

The "book" official is a lot like a soup dish, wide and shallow. He can hold small amounts of anything (trivia) but the slightest jarring (controversy) spills the "soup," usually in someone else's lap.

◆

A "book/mechanic" official on the field may be fast and accurate, but lack judgment. The "experienced" official may be slow and sloppy, but have brilliant judgment. (I'll go with judgment and teach him to dress and hustle.)

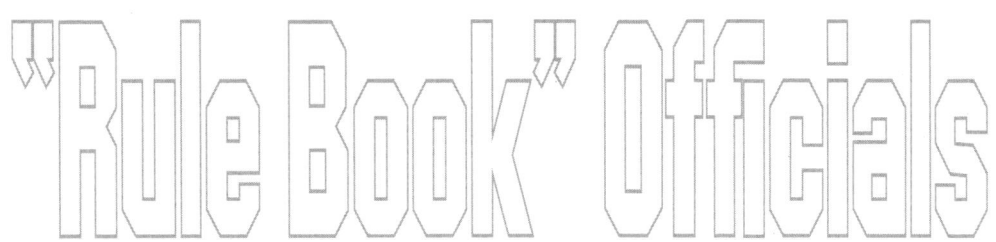

"Rule Book" Officials

How many officials' briefcases, where their rule book hides, should be written, as on the bottles from a drugstore: "For external use only"?

◆

The rule book is the best instant replay practice for those officials who want to get the next similar situation right.

◆

During the post-game discussion, admit your errors before someone two days later exaggerates them to coaches and the supervisor.

◆

In the post-game discussion with the crew and observer, remember several excuses are less convincing than one.

◆

Know the rules, know the game…Ignorance is a voluntary misfortune.

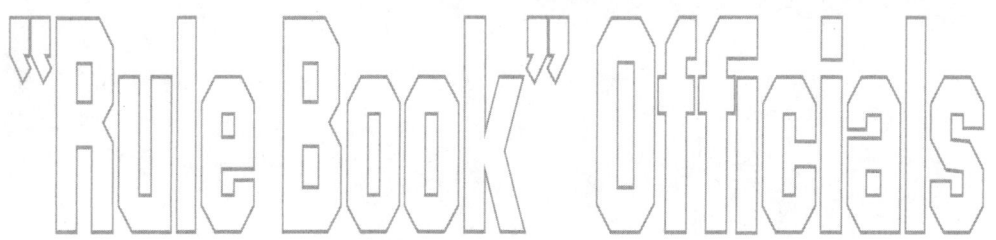

Having a perspective of what is going on in the game, is more valuable than 100% on the last rules test.

◆

Getting 100% correct on a rules test is like correctly naming all of the parts of a gun. Under fire, can you still shoot the game?

◆

The rule bookworm at the pregame knows all the answers, keeps thinking up strange new questions, then swallows his whistle on the opening kick-off.

◆

Reading the rule book vs. applying what you read to the game is the same as knowing how to turn the key to start the car, but having no idea how to drive.

◆

Some book officials are like blotters; they soak it all up, but get it backward.

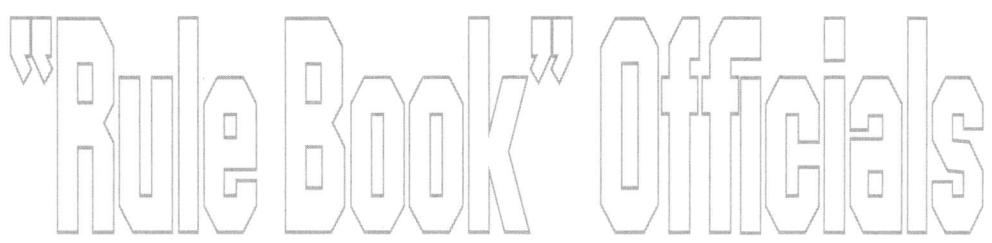

"Rule Book" Officials

Book officials have good aim in the pregame conference and are poor shots after the first kick off.

♦

A book official is like the guy who will spend a half an hour sharpening a knife just so he can whittle a stick.

♦

Book officials might be able to attain wisdom, had they not assumed they already knew everything.

♦

Book officials read enough to stay misinformed.

♦

Book officials memorize the rules and throw away common sense

Section 14
Supervisor Observer/Umpire

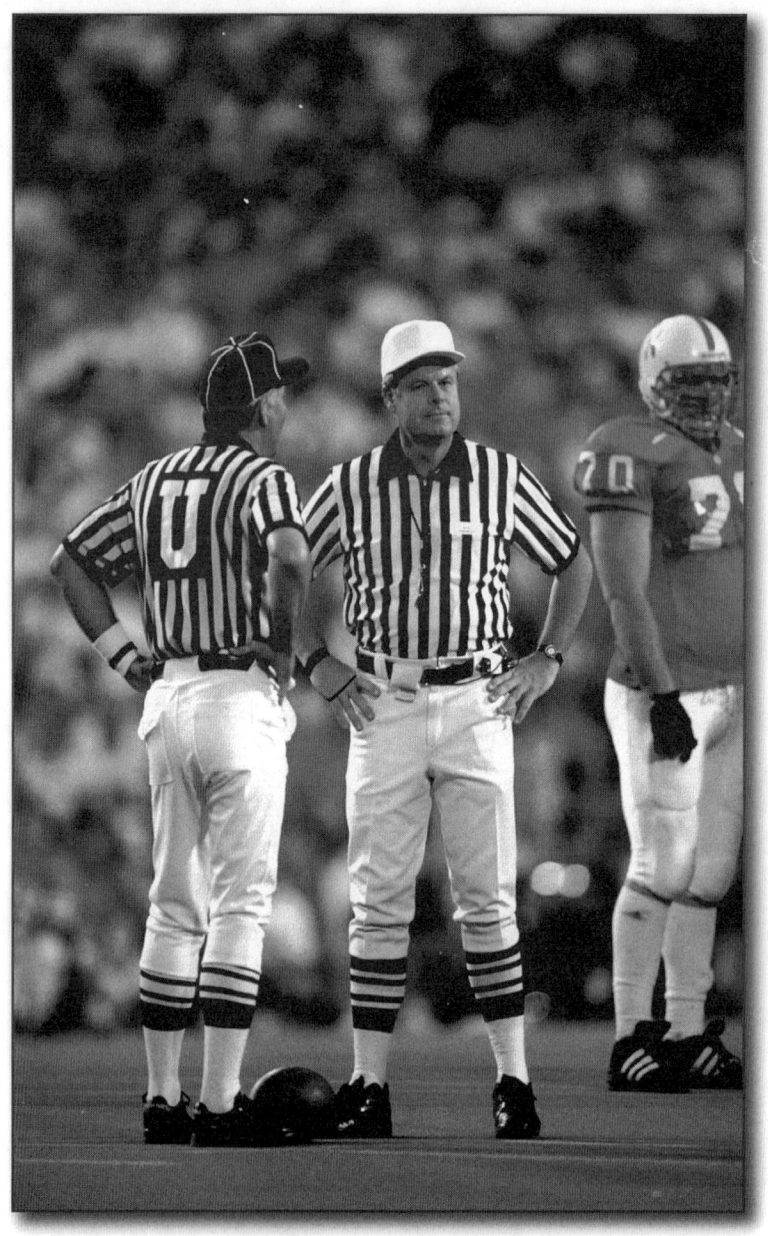

UMPIRE: Richard Whittenburg (U) providing me with "reminders" during a time out at a Nebraska game. I have never seen a referee officiate a great game without an effective umpire...

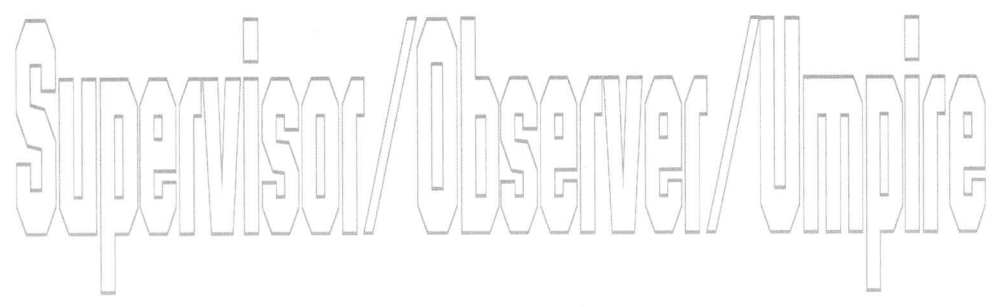

Supervisor/Observer/Umpire

I have the greatest respect for supervisors, observers, and umpires in sports officiating. In fact, since I retired from officiating three years ago, I am beginning this fall my third season, as an Instant Replay Official (that experience might be a book in itself). I have collected basically "tongue-in-cheek quotations poking fun at bosses and constructive "critics" of sports officials.

In my opinion as referee, the referee and umpire actually "run" the game of football. The referee is responsible for communicating and working with the offense, while the umpire has the same responsibility with the defense. The umpire officiates behind the defensive lineman and has the most dangerous position in football as a sports official. It is believed that they are injured four times as often as the other six positions combined. So at the risk of creating some anger among my umpire friends, these are, of course, in jest. This chapter may be appreciated more by sports officials than fans.

> My supervisor told me that I was one year away from being a good official. And the next year, I was two years away.

---◆---

> If you are upset by the criticism of your supervisor, it usually means that you deserved it.

---◆---

> If the new supervisor does not fit the "culture" of the conference, chances are the employees that he brings in won't either.

Supervisor/Observer/Umpire

In the post-game conference, the goal is to have more exclamation points (!) than question marks (?).

———◆———

"My way or the highway" works for the supervisor. "My way is the highway" is usually an official's last season.

———◆———

Having a supervisor praise you when you know you have had a bad game is like having the hangman say you've got a pretty neck. ✓

———◆———

Not the kind of critique you want to hear; "The game was officiated in such a way that it gave failure a bad name."

———◆———

The umpire should be the built in "crap detector." He keeps the "trenches" under control.

Supervisor/Observer/Umpire

No one cares who is pulling the cart until the horse is dead, or the umpire is injured. (No one likes to take his place.)

◆

Just when we learn to "take things with a grain of salt" — The supervisor puts us on a salt-free diet.

◆

An effective supervisor can put his finger on your officiating faults without rubbing it in.

◆

A good football observer must have the tactful ability to have good enough manners to make him indistinguishable from being challenging and direct.

◆

The power of an accurate and efficient observer is commonly called cynicism by those who don't have it and can't take it.

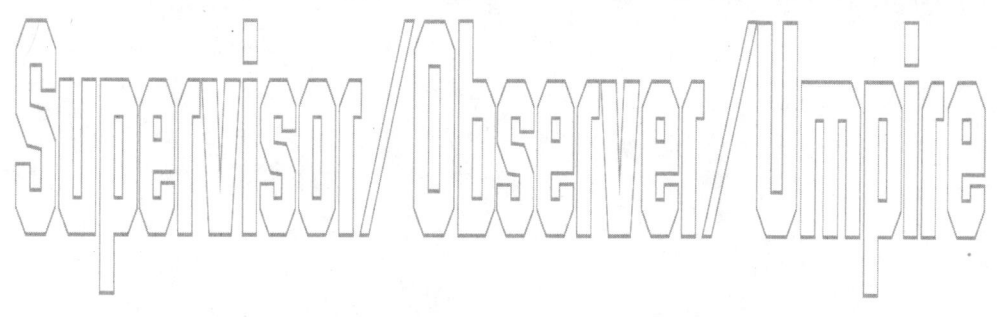

Supervisor/Observer/Umpire

If you believe the past cannot be changed, wait until an observer who doesn't like your "style" writes his report.

◆

The relationship of some observers to an official is that of a knife to a throat.

◆

The ideal football observer is one who has only one arm, so we will never hear "on the other hand."

◆

A poor evaluator is a bundle of biases held together by insecurity and jealousy.

◆

You can't help but like the supervisor of officials because if you don't, he fires you.

◆

It is easier to explain to the supervisor the good game you officiated than to try to explain why you did not.

Supervisor/Observer/Umpire

Whenever an official begs to be treated "fairly" by the supervisor, it is often a sign that they have given up on their potential for achieving excellence.

◆

Three words that will reduce your schedule next year are: could + would + won't.

◆

Some observers come into the locker room after a tough game on the field and then attempt to kill the wounded.

◆

Evaluation is sometimes tough. If you are not big enough for criticism, then you are too small for praise.

◆

Beware of the supervisor who defends the status quo official, when the "quo" (official) has lost his status.

◆

Some officials give their supervisor all of the necessary examples for their own destruction.

Supervisor/Observer/Umpire

There are two kinds of "truths" when confronted by a supervisor after the game: the real truth or the made-up truths. The "phantom" truths will get you fired.

◆

Some observers like to talk about plays, rules and situations that they don't understand, and then try to make you believe it's your fault.

◆

If the umpires will stop telling lies about referees, we (referees) will stop telling the truth about umpires.

◆

Some umpires are so slow, they can't keep up with yesterday.

◆

As you gain experience, except for umpires, the "pickins" get slimmer. (body mass)

◆

Even a large umpire wrapped up in himself is a very small package.

Supervisor/Observer/Umpire

Most umpires had a magnificent build before their stomach went on to a career of its own.

◆

Underneath the flabby exterior of some umpires is an enormous lack of character.

◆

Supervisors comment: "Anyone who talks by the yard and thinks by the inch will be moved by my foot."

◆

It is not the ten minutes it takes umpires to gobble down their food, but it is the "seconds" that gets them in trouble.

◆

A few umpires will lose weight, then get thick and tired of it.

◆

One chop stick at a Chinese restaurant could help a few umpires.

Supervisor/Observer/Umpire

The elastic girdle that umpires wear keeps figures from telling the truth.

◆

The shortest way for umpires to go to the bottom is by over-using the fork.

◆

The skinniest umpires do things they don't like — By eating things they don't like.

◆

You can depend on heavy umpires to never stoop to anything low.

◆

Why is it that supervisors always "pet" their pet peeves?

◆

The happiest time for an umpire is when he finds out that someone on the crew weighs more than him.

Supervisor/Observer/Umpire

After a tough game to officiate, the supervisor doesn't come into your locker room concerned about your "labor pains"…Show him the baby.

◆

Some umpires keep their backs to the wall because they have too much up front.

◆

When your back goes out more than you do, move to the umpire position unless you are the umpire.

◆

When the supervisor gives you "food for thought," you are probably getting a lot of baloney.

◆

Observers need to realize that after a game is not a good time to throw the "kitchen sink and all of the plumbing" at a crew when a few washers will do until the "plumber" calls next week.

Supervisor/Observer/Umpire

If a dentist is your supervisor, don't let him have the ability to extract your nerve and courage to do the right thing on the field.

◆

An observer that agrees with everything you say to him is either a fool or getting ready to fire you.

BOOK CREDITS
(READ AND/OR ENDORSED BOOK)

ACTIVE OFFICIALS

NAME	LOCATION	CONFERENCE	BUSINESS
Jon Bible	Austin, TX	Southwest, Big XII	Law Professor
Richard Brown	Norman, OK	Big XII	Human Resources
Randy Christal	Austin, TX	Southwest, Big XII	P.R. Bus. Officer
Tim Crowley	Austin, TX	Southwest, Big XII	Insurance Exec.
Mike Defee	Groves, TX	Southland, Big XII	Elect. Contractor
Curtis Graham	Shreveport, LA	Big 8, Big XII	Airlines Adm.
Al Green	Columbia, MO	Big 8, Big XII	Coke Cola Exec.
Brad Horchem	Kansas City, KS	Big 8, Big XII	Environmentalist
Don Kapral	Plano, TX	Big 10, Big XII	Sales
Scott Koch	York, NE	Big 8, Big XII	H.S. Principal
Phil Laurie	Topeka, KS	Big 8, Big XII	Sales
Dwight Neibling	Kansas City, KS	Big XII	Chevron, Manager
David Oliver	Topeka, KS	Big 8, Big XII	Banking
Tom Wuick	Kansas City, KS	Big XII	Construction
Rocky Ryan	St. Charles, MO	Big 8, Big XII	Teacher/Coach
Tom Walker	Omaha, NE	Big 8, Big XII	Hospital Adm.
Dwight Widen	St. Ansgar, IA	Big XII	Superintendent
Len Williams	Desoto, TX	Big 8, Big XII	Business Officer
Tom Ahlers	Urbandale, IA	Big 8, Big XII	Medical Care
David Ames	Ft. Collins, CO	Big 8, Big XII	Professor
Gary Brown	Oklahoma City, OK	Big 8, Big XII	Insurance
Don Brown	Oklahoma City, OK	Southwest	College Coach
Paul Brown	Omaha, NE	Big 8	Attorney
Vance Carlson	Ft. Hays, KS	Big 8	Sales
John Davidson	Austin, TX	Southwest, Big XII	Investments

FORMER COLLEGE OFFICIALS

NAME	LOCATION	CONFERENCE	BUSINESS
Frank Gaines	Lincoln, NE	Big 8	IRS
Jim Hatfield	Oklahoma City, OK	Southwest, Big XII	Energy, CEO
Bob Holliday	Des Moines, IA	Big 8, Big XII	Attorney
Dick Honig	E. Lansing, MI	Big 10	Sales
Homer Jackson	Misquite, TX	Big XII	U.S. Postal Service
Jim Jankowski	Waterloo, NE	Big 8, Big XII	Sales
J.C. Leimbach	St. Joseph, MO	Big 8, NFL, Big XII	Teacher
John Lewis	Murphy, TX	Southwest, Big XII	Transprotation
Mike Liner	Lubbock, TX	Southwest, Big XII	Bank Executive
Duane Osborne	Seneca, KS	Big 8, Big XII	H.S. Counselor
Terry Porter	Stillwater, OK	Big 8, Big XII	Sales
Bob Ratliff	Hurst, TX	SW & Southland	IRS
John Robinson	Bountiful, UT	WAC, NFL, Big XII	High School Adm.
Frank Shepard	Liano, TX	Southwest	Business Contractor
Joe Thompson	Pittsburg, TX	OIC & Southwest	Quality Control
Terry Turlington	Kennett, MO	Big 8, Big XII	High School Prin.
Willie Weisbrook	Lincoln, NE	Big 8, Big XII	Sales
Richard Whittenburg	Lubbock, TX	Southwest, Big XII	Banking

ACTIVE NFL OFFICIALS

Bill Corollo
George Hayward
Mark Hittner
Jeff Lamberth
Phil Luckett
Steve Stellges

COACHES

LOCATION WHEN I WAS OFFICIATING:

Pat Jones	Head Coach	Oklahoma State University
John Mackovic	Head Coach	University of Texas
Dan McCarney	Head Coach	Iowa State University
Bill McCartney	Head Coach	University of Colorado
Tom Osborne	Head Coach	University of Nebraska
R.C. Slocum	Head Coach	Texas A&M University
Bill Snyder	Head Coach	Kansas State University

FOOTBALL SUPERVISORS

Walt Anderson, Big XII
Jim Blackwood, WAC Conference
Donnie Duncan, Big 8, Big XII
Bruce Finlayson, Big 8
Tim Millis, Big XII
Mike Pereira, NFL
Red Cashion (retired NFL)

MEDIA

Dave Armstrong, Television Sports Broadcaster
Max Falkenstein, KU Hall of Fame Broadcaster
Blair Kerkhoff, K.C. Star Newspaper, Sports Writer
Ken Koestr, Referee Magazine, Editor
Jason Whitlock, K.C. Star Newspaper, Sports Writer, TV

AUTHOR BIOGRAPHY

Dr. Laurie was an educator for 44 years A high school principal in Topeka, Kansas; Springfield, Missouri; Shawnee Mission, Kansas and Blue Valley, Overland Park, Kansas. He was also an Associate Professor at Emporia State University, Emporia, Kansas.

He was honored as "Missouri High School Principal of the Year" and received the "Alumni Fellow Award for the College of Education" from Kansas State University. Dr. Laurie received his B.S. and PhD degrees from Kansas State University, and his Masters Degree from the University of Colorado.

He developed a block schedule for high schools that is used in over 4000 high schools, as well as, many of our Department of Defense Schools, worldwide. He has presented on this topic in 37 states, Panama, Japan, Belgium and Germany.

His officiating career spans over 40 years. He has officiated Kansas state high school football and basketball. Dr. Laurie officiated small college basketball and football for 20 years. He was a referee in the Big 8 Conference for 13 years, 11 years in the Big XII, and for the past three years an Instant Replay Official for the Big XII Conference. He was also president of both Big 8 and Big XII Football Officials Associations. Dr. Laurie officiated as referee at numerous college championships, as well as the following Bowl games:

Rose Bowl (2), Sugar Bowl, Fiesta Bowl, Peach Bowl (2), Coca Cola Bowl/Japan, Sun Bowl, Aloha Bowl, San Francisco Bowl, Mobile Bowl.

He has been a guest speaker at football and basketball clinics for high school and college officials in several states and foreign countries. He was inducted into the Topeka Officials Hall of Fame and the Kansas Collegiate Officials Hall of Fame. He is the author of several articles appearing in **Referee Magazine** and **American Football Journal**.

He may be reached at johnclaurie@yahoo.com